Full Stack Development With Spring Boot 3 And React

Mastering Modern Web Development with Spring Boot 3 and React: Build Scalable, Dynamic Applications from Frontend to Backend

SIMON TELLIER

Table of Contents

Chapter 1: Introduction to Full-Stack Development

What Full-Stack Development Is All About

Full-stack development refers to the ability to work on both the front end (what users see and interact with) and the back end (the underlying systems, logic, and databases) of an application. A full-stack developer is someone who has the skills to develop and maintain every part of a software application. Whether it's designing a user-friendly interface or building robust server-side functionality, full-stack development combines a wide range of skills into one comprehensive role.

To break it down further, the term "full-stack" encompasses three main components:

1. **Frontend Development**: This involves creating the user-facing side of a web application. It's about designing and implementing user interfaces, ensuring responsiveness, and delivering a seamless experience for users. Technologies like HTML, CSS, and JavaScript form the backbone of front-end development. Modern frameworks like React, Angular, or Vue.js take it a step further by enabling developers to build dynamic, interactive interfaces with ease.

2. **Backend Development**: The backend is where the application's logic, calculations, and database interactions happen. It ensures that the system runs smoothly behind the scenes. Backend development involves working with servers, creating APIs, and managing data storage. Languages like Java, Python, Node.js, and PHP are common in backend development, with frameworks like Spring Boot simplifying complex tasks.

3. **Databases**: A key part of any application is storing, retrieving, and managing data. Databases can be relational (e.g., MySQL, PostgreSQL) or non-relational (e.g., MongoDB). A full-stack developer must understand how to design database schemas, query data efficiently, and maintain data integrity.

Full-stack development is about bridging these three areas. It allows developers to oversee the entire lifecycle of a project, from the initial design to the final deployment. While some developers specialize in either frontend or backend, the demand for full-stack developers has grown significantly. Businesses value individuals who can see the bigger picture and contribute to all parts of a project.

In today's fast-paced tech industry, being a full-stack developer is more than just a skill—it's a mindset. It's about adaptability, problem-solving, and a commitment to delivering a cohesive product. The role is dynamic, challenging, and rewarding, offering endless opportunities to grow and learn.

Why Choose Spring Boot 3 and React

When it comes to full-stack development, choosing the right technologies can make or break a project. Spring Boot 3 and React are a powerful combination that offers flexibility, scalability, and developer efficiency. Let's break down why these two technologies are a perfect fit for modern web development.

1. Spring Boot 3: A Backend Powerhouse

Spring Boot is a framework that simplifies Java-based backend development. Built on top of the Spring Framework, it provides pre-configured setups and tools that eliminate the need for boilerplate code. Spring Boot 3, the latest version, brings several enhancements that make it even more appealing to developers.

- **Ease of Use**: Spring Boot streamlines the process of setting up a backend. With features like auto-configuration and starter dependencies, developers can get a project running quickly without spending hours configuring servers or dependencies.
- **Microservices-Friendly**: As businesses move towards microservices architecture, Spring Boot has become the go-to choice for building scalable, independent services. Its lightweight nature and robust support for REST APIs make it ideal for creating modular systems.
- **Performance and Efficiency**: Spring Boot 3 introduces native support for GraalVM, which allows for faster application startup times and reduced memory usage. This is a game-changer for modern cloud-native applications.
- **Extensive Ecosystem**: The Spring ecosystem includes a vast array of tools for everything from security (Spring Security) to database management (Spring Data).

With Spring Boot, developers have access to a comprehensive toolkit that covers nearly every aspect of backend development.

- **Community and Documentation**: With one of the largest developer communities, Spring Boot offers extensive documentation, tutorials, and community support. This makes it an excellent choice for both beginners and seasoned developers.

2. React: The Frontend Powerhouse

React is a JavaScript library developed by Facebook for building user interfaces. Its declarative approach and component-based architecture have revolutionized frontend development, making it one of the most popular choices among developers.

- **Component-Based Architecture**: React allows developers to build reusable, modular components that can be easily managed and updated. This not only speeds up development but also ensures consistency across the application.
- **Virtual DOM for Speed**: React's Virtual DOM optimizes updates to the user interface, resulting in faster performance and a smoother user experience. It's particularly useful for applications that require frequent updates or have complex UIs.
- **Rich Ecosystem**: From state management tools like Redux and React Context to styling libraries like Material-UI, React's ecosystem provides everything needed to create polished, high-performing applications.
- **Strong Community Support**: React boasts a massive community of developers who actively contribute to its ecosystem. This means access to countless libraries, plugins, and learning resources.
- **Future-Proofing**: React's flexibility and widespread adoption ensure that it remains relevant in the constantly changing tech landscape. Developers can confidently invest in React knowing it's here to stay.

3. Why They Work So Well Together

Spring Boot 3 and React complement each other perfectly, offering a full-stack solution that's both efficient and scalable.

- **Seamless API Integration**: Spring Boot excels at building robust REST APIs, while React makes it easy to consume and display data from those APIs. Together, they enable smooth communication between the frontend and backend.

3

- **Scalability**: Both Spring Boot and React are designed to handle large-scale applications. Whether it's managing thousands of concurrent users or serving dynamic content, this combination can handle the load.
- **Flexibility**: Spring Boot's microservices architecture and React's modular components provide the flexibility needed to adapt to changing business requirements.
- **Developer Productivity**: By combining the simplicity of Spring Boot with the rapid development capabilities of React, developers can build and deploy applications faster than ever before.
- **Cross-Platform Potential**: React's ability to work with React Native extends its capabilities to mobile app development, allowing developers to reuse components and logic.

Choosing Spring Boot 3 and React isn't just about picking popular technologies—it's about choosing tools that are efficient, reliable, and future-ready. Together, they empower developers to build scalable, dynamic applications that deliver exceptional user experiences.

In the chapters ahead, you'll learn how to harness the full potential of these two technologies to become a proficient full-stack developer. From setting up your environment to deploying production-ready applications, this book will guide you through every step of the process. Whether you're new to full-stack development or looking to refine your skills, you'll find everything you need right here. Let's get started!

Tools and Technologies You'll Learn

One of the hallmarks of being a successful full-stack developer is mastering the right set of tools and technologies. Throughout this book, you will gain hands-on experience with industry-standard tools, frameworks, and platforms that are essential for building modern web applications. Here's what you'll work with and learn to use effectively:

---

1. Spring Boot 3

- A backend framework that simplifies Java-based development.
- **Key Features You'll Explore:**
  - REST API development.
  - Spring Security for authentication and authorization.
  - Database integration using Spring Data JPA.
  - Application monitoring with Spring Boot Actuator.
  - GraalVM integration for performance optimization.

2. React

- A JavaScript library for building user interfaces.
- **Key Features You'll Explore:**
  - Building reusable components.
  - Managing application state with React Context and Redux Toolkit.
  - Using React Router for navigation.
  - Styling with TailwindCSS and Material-UI.
  - Optimizing performance with lazy loading and code splitting.

3. Database Management Systems

- Learn to design, query, and manage data with relational and non-relational databases:
  - **Relational**: MySQL or PostgreSQL for structured data.
  - **Non-Relational**: MongoDB for flexible, JSON-based document storage.
- Explore database connection pooling, query optimization, and schema design.

4. API Communication

- Use tools and libraries for frontend-backend communication:
  - Axios for handling HTTP requests in React.
  - RESTful API principles for building robust backend services.

○ Tools for testing APIs like Postman.

---

5. Docker

- Learn containerization for packaging and deploying applications.
- Key concepts include creating Dockerfiles, managing containers, and using Docker Compose for multi-service applications.

---

6. Build Tools

- Automate tasks and streamline workflows with tools like:
    ○ **Maven/Gradle**: Dependency management for Spring Boot.
    ○ **Webpack and Vite**: Bundling and optimizing React applications.

---

7. Testing Frameworks

- Write reliable, maintainable tests to ensure code quality:
    ○ **Spring Boot**: Use JUnit and Mockito for backend testing.
    ○ **React**: Leverage Jest and React Testing Library for frontend unit and integration tests.

---

8. Deployment Platforms

- Learn to deploy applications to the cloud using:
    ○ AWS Elastic Beanstalk for backend services.
    ○ Vercel or Netlify for hosting React applications.
    ○ Kubernetes for managing containerized applications.

---

9. Continuous Integration and Deployment (CI/CD)

- Automate development workflows using:
  - GitHub Actions for CI/CD pipelines.
  - Automated builds, tests, and deployments.

---

10. Monitoring and Debugging

- Tools like Spring Boot Actuator for monitoring backend performance.
- Browser developer tools and React DevTools for debugging the frontend.
- Logging frameworks like SLF4J and Logback.

This comprehensive toolset ensures that by the end of the book, you'll not only know how to build full-stack applications but also how to maintain, test, optimize, and deploy them with confidence.

Setting Expectations for This Book

This book is designed to be your step-by-step guide to mastering full-stack development with Spring Boot 3 and React. It caters to developers at different stages of their journey, providing a balance of foundational knowledge, practical application, and advanced concepts. Here's what you can expect:

---

1. Hands-On Learning

- This book emphasizes practical, project-based learning. Each chapter builds on the last, culminating in complete, deployable applications.
- Expect to write code as you follow along. You'll learn by doing, solving real-world challenges, and creating solutions you can showcase in your portfolio.

---

2. No Prior Full-Stack Experience Required

- While some basic programming knowledge will help, this book is written with beginners in mind. Concepts are explained in a clear and accessible way.
- Intermediate and advanced developers will also benefit from best practices, optimization techniques, and deep dives into advanced topics.

---

3. Progressive Learning

- The content is structured to guide you from the basics to advanced concepts:
  - Early chapters focus on building foundational knowledge.
  - Later chapters introduce more complex features like performance optimization, deployment, and real-time capabilities.
- By the end, you'll have built several full-stack applications, from simple prototypes to advanced, production-ready systems.

---

4. Real-World Applications

- You'll work on three complete projects:
  - **E-Commerce Application**: A platform with products, carts, and checkout features.
  - **Blog Platform**: A dynamic content management system.
  - **Social Media Dashboard**: A feature-rich app with real-time notifications.
- Each project is designed to reflect common industry scenarios, preparing you to tackle similar challenges in your career.

---

5. Focus on Best Practices

- Beyond just writing code, this book teaches you how to write **good code**. You'll learn:
  - Clean, maintainable design patterns for both frontend and backend.
  - Proper error handling and debugging techniques.
  - Security practices for building safe applications.

6. Tools for Career Advancement

- Full-stack development is a high-demand skill. By mastering the content in this book, you'll be equipped to:
    - Build your portfolio with impressive projects.
    - Ace technical interviews with a deep understanding of backend and frontend concepts.
    - Work efficiently in professional, collaborative environments.

7. Long-Term Learning

- Technologies like Spring Boot and React are widely used and constantly evolving. This book gives you the foundation to keep learning and adapting as these tools grow.
- You'll also gain a problem-solving mindset, making it easier to adopt new frameworks and technologies in the future.

This book isn't just about teaching you how to code—it's about helping you grow as a developer. Whether you're looking to start your full-stack development journey, switch careers, or level up your skills, this book will serve as a valuable resource every step of the way. Let's dive in!

Chapter 2: Setting Up Your Development Environment

A well-configured development environment is the foundation of any successful software project. In this chapter, we'll walk through the process of installing and configuring the essential tools you'll need for full-stack development with Spring Boot and React. By the end of this chapter, you'll have everything set up to start building robust applications.

Installing and Configuring Java

Spring Boot is built on Java, so the first step is to ensure you have Java installed on your system. For this book, we'll use **Java Development Kit (JDK) 17**, as it's a long-term support (LTS) version and compatible with Spring Boot 3.

Step 1: Downloading the JDK

1. **Visit the official website**:
   Go to the Adoptium or Oracle JDK page and download JDK 17 for your operating system (Windows, macOS, or Linux).
2. **Choose the appropriate installer**:
   - For Windows: Download the .exe file.
   - For macOS: Download the .dmg file.
   - For Linux: Use the .tar.gz file or your distribution's package manager.

Step 2: Installing the JDK

1. **On Windows**:
   - Run the .exe file and follow the installation wizard.
   - During installation, ensure the **"Set JAVA_HOME"** option is selected.

2. **On macOS**:
   - ○ Double-click the .dmg file and follow the instructions.
   - ○ After installation, verify it by running java -version in the terminal.
3. **On Linux**:
   - ○ Extract the .tar.gz file to a directory like /opt.
   - ○ Add the JAVA_HOME environment variable to your shell configuration file (e.g., .bashrc or .zshrc).

Step 3: Configuring Environment Variables

1. **Set JAVA_HOME**:
   - ○ On Windows:
     - ■ Go to *System Properties > Advanced > Environment Variables*.
     - ■ Add a new variable called JAVA_HOME and set its value to the path where Java is installed.
   - ○ On macOS/Linux:

Open your terminal and add this line to your shell configuration file:

bash

CopyEdit

```
export JAVA_HOME=/path/to/java
export PATH=$JAVA_HOME/bin:$PATH
```

- ■
  - ■ Reload the configuration file by running source ~/.bashrc or source ~/.zshrc.

Verify the installation:

Open a terminal or command prompt and type:

bash

CopyEdit

```
java -version
```

You should see output similar to this:

scss

CopyEdit

java version "17.x.x"

Java(TM) SE Runtime Environment

Java HotSpot(TM) 64-Bit Server VM

Installing and Configuring Spring Boot

Spring Boot simplifies Java backend development, and installing it is straightforward.

Step 1: Installing Spring Boot CLI

While you don't need the Spring Boot CLI to follow this book, it's helpful for quickly creating and testing applications.

1. Download the Spring Boot CLI using a package manager:

On macOS:

bash

CopyEdit

brew install springboot

On Linux (with SDKMAN):

bash

CopyEdit

curl -s "https://get.sdkman.io" | bash

source "$HOME/.sdkman/bin/sdkman-init.sh"

sdk install springboot

- On Windows: Use the official Spring Boot distribution from the Spring website.

Verify the installation by typing:

bash

CopyEdit

spring --version

2. You should see the Spring Boot version displayed.

Step 2: Setting Up a Spring Boot Project

1. Go to the **Spring Initializr** at start.spring.io.
2. Fill in the project details:
   - **Project**: Maven (preferred) or Gradle.
   - **Language**: Java.
   - **Spring Boot Version**: 3.x.x.
   - **Dependencies**: Add the following:
     - Spring Web (for REST APIs).
     - Spring Data JPA (for database interaction).
     - Spring Security (for authentication).
     - H2 or PostgreSQL (for database integration).
3. Click **Generate** to download the project as a .zip file.
4. Extract the .zip file and open it in your favorite IDE (we'll set up IntelliJ IDEA in the next section).

Installing and Configuring IntelliJ IDEA

IntelliJ IDEA is one of the most popular Integrated Development Environments (IDEs) for Java development, offering robust tools for working with Spring Boot.

Step 1: Downloading IntelliJ IDEA

1. Go to the JetBrains website.
2. Choose the **Community Edition** (free) or **Ultimate Edition** (paid, includes advanced Spring tools).

Step 2: Installing IntelliJ IDEA

1. Download the installer for your operating system:

- o Windows: .exe file.
- o macOS: .dmg file.
- o Linux: .tar.gz file.
2. Run the installer and follow the on-screen instructions.
3. Launch IntelliJ IDEA once installed.

Step 3: Configuring IntelliJ IDEA

1. **Install Plugins**:
   - o Go to *File > Settings > Plugins*.
   - o Search for and install the **Spring Boot** and **Lombok** plugins (Lombok is often used in Spring Boot projects for reducing boilerplate code).
2. **Open Your Spring Boot Project**:
   - o Go to *File > Open* and select the folder containing your Spring Boot project.
   - o IntelliJ will automatically import the project and download all required dependencies.
3. **Run Your Application**:
   - o Open the Application.java file in your project.
   - o Right-click and select **Run**. You should see a message in the console indicating that the Spring Boot application has started successfully.

Step 4: Customizing IntelliJ IDEA for Productivity

1. **Code Style and Formatting**:
   - o Go to *File > Settings > Code Style* and configure it to match Java conventions.
2. **Enable Live Templates**:
   - o Use shortcuts to generate common code snippets.
3. **Version Control Integration**:
   - o Connect IntelliJ IDEA to your GitHub or GitLab account for version control.

At this stage, you've set up Java, Spring Boot, and IntelliJ IDEA, and you're ready to start developing your backend. Next, we'll move on to setting up Node.js, React, and Visual Studio Code for frontend development. Stay tuned for the next step in your full-stack journey!

Setting Up Node.js, React, and Visual Studio Code

Setting Up Node.js

Node.js is essential for building and running React applications. It allows developers to work with JavaScript on the server side and provides a runtime environment for JavaScript outside the browser. Additionally, the Node Package Manager (NPM) is bundled with Node.js, enabling the installation of libraries and tools.

Step 1: Downloading Node.js

1. **Visit the official Node.js website**:
   Go to https://nodejs.org.
2. **Select the appropriate version**:
   - Choose the **LTS (Long-Term Support)** version for stability and reliability.
   - Avoid using the Current version unless you need cutting-edge features.
3. **Download the installer**:
   - Windows: Download the .msi file.
   - macOS: Download the .pkg file.
   - Linux: Use your package manager or download the .tar.gz file.

Step 2: Installing Node.js

1. **Run the installer**:
   - Follow the instructions in the installation wizard.
   - Ensure that the option to install NPM is selected.
2. **Verify the installation**:

Open a terminal or command prompt and type:

bash

CopyEdit

```
node -v
npm -v
```

- You should see the versions of Node.js and NPM displayed.

Step 3: Configuring NPM

Check the global installation directory:

bash

CopyEdit

```
npm config get prefix
```

1. Ensure it points to a directory accessible to your user account.

Update NPM (optional):

bash

CopyEdit

```
npm install -g npm@latest
```

2. This updates NPM to the latest stable version.

Setting Up React

React is a JavaScript library for building user interfaces. To get started, we'll use Create React App (CRA), a tool that sets up a new React project with minimal configuration.

Step 1: Creating a React Project

1. Open a terminal and navigate to the directory where you want to create your project.

Run the following command to create a new React application:

bash

CopyEdit

```
npx create-react-app my-app
```

2. Replace my-app with the desired name for your project.

Once the setup is complete, navigate to the project directory:

bash

CopyEdit

```
cd my-app
```

3.

Start the development server to verify everything is working:

bash

CopyEdit

```
npm start
```

4. This will launch your React application in the browser at http://localhost:3000.

Step 2: Installing Additional Libraries Depending on your project's needs, you may want to install some common libraries:

React Router for navigation:

bash

CopyEdit

```
npm install react-router-dom
```

- **State Management** (optional):

Context API is built into React, but you can also use Redux Toolkit for larger applications:

bash

CopyEdit

```
npm install @reduxjs/toolkit react-redux
```

17

Setting Up Visual Studio Code

Visual Studio Code (VS Code) is a lightweight and powerful code editor with robust support for JavaScript and React.

Step 1: Downloading VS Code

1. Visit the official VS Code website.
2. Download the installer for your operating system (Windows, macOS, or Linux).

Step 2: Installing VS Code

1. Run the installer and follow the on-screen instructions.
2. Launch VS Code after installation.

Step 3: Configuring VS Code

1. **Install Extensions**:
   - React Development: Install the **ES7+ React/Redux/React-Native snippets** extension.
   - Formatting: Install **Prettier** for consistent code formatting.
   - Linting: Install **ESLint** to catch errors and enforce coding standards.
   - Docker: Install the **Docker extension** if you'll be using Docker.
2. **Configure Settings**:
   - Go to *File > Preferences > Settings*.
   - Enable auto-formatting on save:
     Search for format on save and check the box.
3. **Keyboard Shortcuts**:
   Customize shortcuts for actions you use frequently, like running scripts or debugging.
4. **Version Control**:
   - If you're using Git, install the **GitLens** extension to enhance Git integration.

At this stage, your development environment for React is ready to go. Next, let's explore Docker for creating full-stack applications.

Introduction to Docker for Full-Stack Applications

Docker is a powerful tool for creating, managing, and deploying containerized applications. It allows developers to package applications and their dependencies into containers, ensuring consistent behavior across development, testing, and production environments.

What Is Docker?

Docker is a platform that uses containerization to run applications in isolated environments. A **container** is a lightweight, standalone package that includes everything needed to run a piece of software, such as code, runtime, libraries, and system tools.

Why Use Docker for Full-Stack Development?

1. **Environment Consistency**: Containers ensure that applications run the same way regardless of where they are deployed.
2. **Simplified Deployment**: Docker eliminates the "works on my machine" problem by bundling all dependencies.
3. **Scalability**: Containers can be scaled horizontally to handle large workloads.
4. **Easy Collaboration**: Developers can share Docker images, making it easier to work on the same project.

Installing Docker

1. **Download Docker Desktop**:
   Visit Docker's website and download Docker Desktop for your operating system.
2. **Install Docker**:

- ○ Follow the on-screen instructions during installation.
- ○ On macOS and Windows, Docker Desktop runs in the system tray.
- ○ On Linux, follow your distribution's instructions to install Docker Engine.

Verify the Installation:

Open a terminal and type:

bash

CopyEdit

```
docker --version
```

3. You should see the installed Docker version.

Basic Docker Commands

Run a Container:

bash

CopyEdit

```
docker run hello-world
```

1. This command pulls the hello-world image from Docker Hub and runs it, verifying your Docker installation.

List Running Containers:

bash

CopyEdit

```
docker ps
```

2. **Stop a Container**:

   bash

   CopyEdit

   ```
   docker stop <container_id>
   ```

3. **Remove a Container**:

   bash

   CopyEdit

   ```
   docker rm <container_id>
   ```

Creating Docker Containers for Full-Stack Applications

1. Backend with Spring Boot:

Create a Dockerfile in your Spring Boot project directory:

dockerfile

CopyEdit

```
FROM openjdk:17-jdk-slim
VOLUME /tmp
ARG JAR_FILE=target/app.jar
COPY ${JAR_FILE} app.jar
ENTRYPOINT ["java","-jar","/app.jar"]
```

- Build the Docker image:

  bash

  CopyEdit

  ```
  docker build -t spring-boot-app .
  ```

- Run the container:

  bash

  CopyEdit

  ```
  docker run -p 8080:8080 spring-boot-app
  ```

2. Frontend with React:

Create a Dockerfile in your React project directory:

dockerfile

CopyEdit

```
FROM node:18
WORKDIR /app
COPY . .
RUN npm install
RUN npm run build
CMD ["npx", "serve", "-s", "build"]
```

EXPOSE 3000

   ○ Build and run the React container:

   bash

   CopyEdit

   docker build -t react-app .

docker run -p 3000:3000 react-app

With Docker, you can run your Spring Boot backend and React frontend as containers, ensuring they function consistently across environments. In the next chapter, we'll dive deeper into building and configuring your backend with Spring Boot.

Chapter 3: Spring Boot Fundamentals

Overview of Spring Framework and Spring Boot

Spring Framework and Spring Boot are two cornerstones of modern Java development, widely used to build scalable, maintainable, and robust applications. Understanding their relationship and core features is essential for any developer diving into backend development.

What Is Spring Framework?

Spring Framework is a comprehensive open-source framework for building enterprise-grade Java applications. Introduced in 2003, it revolutionized Java development by providing a solution to the complexity of enterprise-level applications. Before Spring, Java development often involved writing a lot of boilerplate code for tasks such as managing dependencies, database transactions, or web requests. Spring simplified this process, offering developers a more streamlined, modular approach.

Core Features of Spring Framework

1. **Inversion of Control (IoC)**
   - IoC is at the heart of Spring Framework. It decouples the components of an application, making them more testable and easier to manage.
   - IoC is implemented via the **Dependency Injection (DI)** mechanism, where objects are injected into a class by the framework instead of being instantiated manually.
   - Example: Instead of manually creating a database service in your application, Spring injects it automatically based on your configuration.
2. **Aspect-Oriented Programming (AOP)**
   - AOP allows developers to separate cross-cutting concerns (e.g., logging, security) from business logic.
   - Instead of cluttering your code with repetitive functionality, you can define these concerns as aspects and apply them declaratively.

23

3. **Transaction Management**
   - Spring provides robust support for managing database transactions. It integrates seamlessly with popular databases and ORM tools like Hibernate.
   - Developers can control transactions declaratively using annotations such as @Transactional.

4. **Spring MVC**
   - Spring's Model-View-Controller (MVC) architecture simplifies web development by separating concerns:
     - **Model**: Manages data and business logic.
     - **View**: Handles the user interface.
     - **Controller**: Handles incoming requests and updates the model or view.
   - Spring MVC enables building RESTful APIs and traditional web applications efficiently.

5. **Integration with Other Frameworks**
   - Spring works well with third-party libraries and tools, including Hibernate (for ORM), Quartz (for scheduling), and more.
   - It's flexible enough to be adapted to a variety of application types, from simple command-line apps to complex microservices.

6. **Modular Architecture**
   - Spring is designed as a collection of modules, so you only use the parts you need.
   - Key modules include:
     - **Spring Core**: Dependency injection and IoC container.
     - **Spring Data**: Data access and integration with databases.
     - **Spring Security**: Authentication and authorization.
     - **Spring Web**: MVC and REST web services.

Challenges with Spring Framework

While Spring Framework is powerful, it comes with its challenges:

1. **Boilerplate Code**: Early versions of Spring required extensive XML configuration files, making setup tedious and error-prone.

2. **Complexity**: Managing dependencies and configurations could become overwhelming in large projects.
3. **Startup Time**: Applications built with Spring often had longer startup times, particularly in development environments.

What Is Spring Boot?

Spring Boot was introduced in 2014 as an extension of Spring Framework to address many of its shortcomings. It simplifies the process of creating Spring-based applications by offering convention-over-configuration and default setups. With Spring Boot, developers can create production-ready applications quickly, without having to deal with extensive boilerplate code.

Key Features of Spring Boot

1. **Auto-Configuration**
   - Spring Boot automatically configures your application based on the dependencies included in your project.
   - For example, if you add spring-boot-starter-data-jpa as a dependency, Spring Boot configures JPA, Hibernate, and database connections without additional setup.
2. **Starter Dependencies**
   - Spring Boot introduces the concept of "starters," which bundle related dependencies into a single package.
   - Example starters:
     - spring-boot-starter-web: Includes dependencies for building web applications.
     - spring-boot-starter-data-jpa: Includes Hibernate and database-related dependencies.
     - spring-boot-starter-security: Includes Spring Security.
3. **Embedded Servers**
   - Spring Boot comes with built-in support for embedded servers like Tomcat, Jetty, and Undertow.

This eliminates the need for external servers, allowing applications to run as standalone JAR files with a simple command:

bash

CopyEdit

```
java -jar application.jar
```

4. **Spring Boot CLI**
   - A command-line tool that allows developers to create and run Spring Boot applications with minimal effort.

Example:

bash

CopyEdit

```
spring init --dependencies=web,data-jpa myapp
```

5. **Actuator**
   - Spring Boot Actuator provides monitoring and management endpoints for applications.
   - Examples of endpoints:
     - /health: Displays the health status of the application.
     - /metrics: Shows application metrics like memory usage and active threads.

6. **Externalized Configuration**
   - Spring Boot supports externalized configuration through property files (application.properties or application.yml) or environment variables.
   - This makes it easy to manage configurations for different environments (e.g., development, testing, production).

7. **Microservices Support**
   - Spring Boot is ideal for building microservices, with support for REST APIs, distributed tracing, and circuit breakers (via Spring Cloud).

8. **Developer Productivity**
   - Spring Boot simplifies repetitive tasks and reduces development time.
   - It integrates seamlessly with modern tools and practices like Docker, Kubernetes, and CI/CD pipelines.

How Spring Boot Works with Spring Framework

Spring Boot is not a replacement for Spring Framework—it's an extension that builds on top of it. It simplifies the setup and development process while retaining all the power and flexibility of the core Spring Framework.

- **Spring Framework** provides the foundation, offering IoC, AOP, and a modular architecture.
- **Spring Boot** enhances this foundation with auto-configuration, embedded servers, and developer-friendly features.

For example, when building a REST API with Spring Framework, you might need to:

1. Configure the DispatcherServlet in a web.xml file.
2. Manually set up dependencies for Jackson (JSON serialization) and Tomcat.
3. Write multiple configuration classes to set up Spring MVC.

With Spring Boot, all of this is handled automatically. You simply include the spring-boot-starter-web dependency, and Spring Boot takes care of the rest.

Why Choose Spring Boot 3?

Spring Boot 3 brings significant improvements over its predecessors. Here's what makes it stand out:

1. **GraalVM Native Support**
   - Spring Boot 3 applications can be compiled into native executables using GraalVM, resulting in faster startup times and reduced memory usage.
   - This is particularly beneficial for serverless and cloud-native applications.
2. **Improved Observability**
   - Built-in support for Micrometer and OpenTelemetry makes monitoring and tracing easier.
3. **Enhanced Security**
   - Better integration with modern authentication protocols like OAuth 2.1.
   - Simplified configurations for securing APIs.

4. **Java 17 Compatibility**
   ○ Leverages the latest features of Java 17, such as records, sealed classes, and new garbage collection algorithms.
5. **Cloud-Native Ready**
   ○ Optimized for Kubernetes and Docker environments.

Spring Framework laid the groundwork for enterprise-grade Java development, but Spring Boot has taken it to the next level by making it simpler, faster, and more developer-friendly. Together, they provide a powerful toolkit for building scalable, maintainable applications, whether you're working on a monolithic system or a suite of microservices.

In the next section, we'll dive into the details of building a backend with Spring Boot, starting with creating your first REST API. Get ready to roll up your sleeves and start coding!

Building Your First Spring Boot Application

Spring Boot makes it incredibly easy to get started with Java-based backend development. In this section, we'll guide you through building your first Spring Boot application, covering everything from setting up the project to running your application locally.

Step 1: Create a Spring Boot Project

To create a Spring Boot application, you can use the Spring Initializr, which provides a quick and easy way to set up your project.

Using Spring Initializr via the Web Interface

1. Open your browser and go to https://start.spring.io.
2. Configure your project settings:
   ○ **Project**: Maven (default) or Gradle (if you prefer Gradle).
   ○ **Language**: Java.
   ○ **Spring Boot Version**: 3.x.x (latest stable version).
   ○ **Group**: com.example (your organization or domain).

- ○ **Artifact**: demo (the name of your application).
- ○ **Name**: demo (same as the artifact name).
- ○ **Dependencies**: Add the following:
  - ■ **Spring Web**: To build REST APIs.
  - ■ **Spring Boot DevTools**: For live reloading during development.
  - ■ **Spring Data JPA**: For database integration.
  - ■ **H2 Database**: An in-memory database for testing.
3. Click **Generate** to download the project as a .zip file.
4. Extract the .zip file to a directory of your choice.

Using Spring Initializr via IntelliJ IDEA

1. Open IntelliJ IDEA and select **New Project**.
2. Choose **Spring Initializr** from the project types.
3. Configure the project settings as described above.
4. Click **Next**, select the required dependencies, and finish the setup. IntelliJ will automatically import the project and download the necessary dependencies.

Step 2: Understand the Project Structure

Once your project is created, you'll see the following structure:

- src/main/java: Contains your application code.
  - ○ com.example.demo: The default package for your classes.
  - ○ DemoApplication.java: The main entry point for your application.
- src/main/resources: Contains configuration files.
  - ○ application.properties: The default configuration file for your application.
- pom.xml: The Maven build file, which lists your dependencies.

29

Step 3: Write Your First REST API

Open the DemoApplication.java **file. You'll see the following code:**
java
CopyEdit
package com.example.demo;

import org.springframework.boot.SpringApplication;

import org.springframework.boot.autoconfigure.SpringBootApplication;

@SpringBootApplication

public class DemoApplication {

  public static void main(String[] args) {

    SpringApplication.run(DemoApplication.class, args);

  }

}

1.
    o **@SpringBootApplication**: This annotation combines three key annotations:
        ▪ **@Configuration**: Indicates that this class contains Spring
           configuration.
        ▪ **@EnableAutoConfiguration**: Enables Spring Boot's
           auto-configuration features.
        ▪ **@ComponentScan**: Scans for Spring components in the specified
           package.

Create a new controller class named HelloController:

java

CopyEdit

```java
package com.example.demo;


import org.springframework.web.bind.annotation.GetMapping;

import org.springframework.web.bind.annotation.RestController;


@RestController

public class HelloController {


    @GetMapping("/hello")

    public String sayHello() {

        return "Hello, Spring Boot!";

    }

}
```

    2.

-        ○ **@RestController**: Marks this class as a REST controller, where each method returns data directly (instead of rendering a view).
-        ○ **@GetMapping**: Maps HTTP GET requests to the sayHello method.

    3. Run your application by right-clicking the DemoApplication class and selecting **Run DemoApplication**.

Open your browser and navigate to http://localhost:8080/hello. You should see the message:

CopyEdit

Hello, Spring Boot!

Core Spring Boot Features and Annotations

Spring Boot offers several features and annotations that simplify application development. Let's explore some of the most important ones.

1. Dependency Injection and Component Scanning

Spring Boot automatically scans your project for components, services, and controllers, thanks to the @ComponentScan annotation.

- **Annotations for Components**:
  - **@Component**: Marks a class as a Spring-managed component.
  - **@Service**: A specialized @Component for business logic.
  - **@Repository**: A specialized @Component for data access.

Example:

java
CopyEdit

```
@Service
public class MyService {
    public String process() {
        return "Processed data";
    }
}


@RestController
```

```
public class MyController {

    private final MyService myService;

    public MyController(MyService myService) {
        this.myService = myService;
    }

    @GetMapping("/process")
    public String process() {
        return myService.process();
    }
}
```

-

---

2. REST API Development

Spring Boot simplifies REST API development with the following annotations:

- **@RestController**: Combines @Controller and @ResponseBody for returning data directly.
- **@RequestMapping**: Maps a class or method to a specific URL.
- **@GetMapping, @PostMapping, @PutMapping, @DeleteMapping**: Shortcuts for mapping HTTP methods.

---

3. Configuration Management

Spring Boot's externalized configuration allows you to manage properties in a central file (application.properties or application.yml).

Example:
properties
CopyEdit

```
server.port=9090

spring.datasource.url=jdbc:h2:mem:testdb
```

- **@Value Annotation**: Injects values from the configuration file into your code.
  java
  CopyEdit

  ```
  @Value("${server.port}")

  private int serverPort;
  ```

---

4. Error Handling

Spring Boot provides built-in error handling and customizable error responses.

Global Exception Handling: Use @ControllerAdvice to handle exceptions globally.
java
CopyEdit

```
@ControllerAdvice

public class GlobalExceptionHandler {


  @ExceptionHandler(RuntimeException.class)

  public ResponseEntity<String> handleRuntimeException(RuntimeException ex) {

    return ResponseEntity.status(HttpStatus.INTERNAL_SERVER_ERROR)
```

```
                              .body("An error occurred: " + ex.getMessage());

    }

}
```

---

5. Spring Boot Starters

Starters simplify dependency management by bundling related libraries.

- Example Starters:
    - spring-boot-starter-web: For web and REST API development.
    - spring-boot-starter-data-jpa: For database interaction using JPA and Hibernate.
    - spring-boot-starter-security: For authentication and authorization.

---

6. Actuator

Spring Boot Actuator provides endpoints for monitoring and managing your application.

Enable Actuator in application.properties:

properties

CopyEdit

management.endpoints.web.exposure.include=*

- Common Actuator Endpoints:
    - /actuator/health: Displays the application's health status.
    - /actuator/metrics: Shows application metrics like memory usage.

---

7. Spring Boot Testing Annotations

Spring Boot simplifies testing with annotations like:

- @SpringBootTest: Loads the full application context for integration testing.

- **@MockBean**: Creates mock objects for dependencies.

Example:

java

CopyEdit

```
@SpringBootTest

public class MyServiceTest {


    @Autowired

    private MyService myService;


    @Test

    public void testProcess() {

        String result = myService.process();

        assertEquals("Processed data", result);

    }

}
```

With these features and annotations, Spring Boot reduces the complexity of Java development, allowing developers to focus on writing business logic. In the next chapter, we'll explore how to integrate databases using Spring Data JPA.

Chapter 4: Building the Backend with Spring Boot

Creating REST APIs with Spring Boot

REST (Representational State Transfer) APIs are at the heart of modern web development, enabling communication between clients (frontend or other services) and servers. Spring Boot simplifies REST API development by providing a powerful framework to build and expose APIs quickly and efficiently. In this chapter, we'll cover the fundamentals of creating REST APIs using Spring Boot, complete with examples and best practices.

What is a REST API?

A REST API allows communication between systems using standard HTTP methods like GET, POST, PUT, and DELETE. It's designed to be stateless, scalable, and platform-independent, making it a popular choice for building web services. REST APIs exchange data in lightweight formats like JSON or XML, with JSON being the most commonly used.

Setting Up Your REST API Project

1. **Create a Spring Boot Project**:
   - Use Spring Initializr to set up a project with the following dependencies:
     - **Spring Web**: For building RESTful web services.
     - **Spring Boot DevTools**: For live reloading during development.
     - **Spring Data JPA**: For database interaction (optional in this step, but useful for later).
     - **H2 Database**: An in-memory database for testing.
2. **Project Structure**: Your project will include the following key files:
   - DemoApplication.java: The main application class.

- A controller class to handle API requests.
- (Optional) A service and repository layer for business logic and data access.

Building Your First REST API

Let's build a simple REST API to manage a list of books.

Step 1: Create a Controller

A controller handles incoming HTTP requests and sends responses back to the client.

Create a class named BookController in the com.example.demo package:

java

CopyEdit

```
package com.example.demo;

import org.springframework.web.bind.annotation.GetMapping;
import org.springframework.web.bind.annotation.PostMapping;
import org.springframework.web.bind.annotation.RequestBody;
import org.springframework.web.bind.annotation.RestController;

import java.util.ArrayList;
import java.util.List;

@RestController
public class BookController {

    private final List<String> books = new ArrayList<>();

    @GetMapping("/books")
    public List<String> getBooks() {
        return books;
    }
```

```
@PostMapping("/books")
public String addBook(@RequestBody String book) {
    books.add(book);
    return "Book added: " + book;
}
}
```

1. **Explanation**:
   - **@RestController**: Marks the class as a REST controller.
   - **@GetMapping("/books")**: Maps GET requests to /books to return the list of books.
   - **@PostMapping("/books")**: Maps POST requests to /books to add a book to the list.
   - **@RequestBody**: Reads JSON input from the request body and maps it to a method parameter.

Step 2: Run and Test the API

1. Start your application by running DemoApplication.java.
2. Open Postman, curl, or your browser to test the endpoints:

GET /books:
bash
CopyEdit
curl -X GET http://localhost:8080/books
Response:
json
CopyEdit
[]

- **POST /books**:
  bash
  CopyEdit
  curl -X POST -H "Content-Type: application/json" -d "\"Spring Boot Essentials\"" http://localhost:8080/books

Response:
yaml
CopyEdit
Book added: Spring Boot Essentials

- **GET /books** (again):
  bash
  CopyEdit
  curl -X GET http://localhost:8080/books

Response:
json
CopyEdit
["Spring Boot Essentials"]

Creating a Complete REST API with CRUD

Let's enhance our API by adding support for Create, Read, Update, and Delete (CRUD) operations on books.

Step 1: Define a Model

Create a Book class to represent the data structure:

java
CopyEdit
```java
package com.example.demo;

public class Book {
    private Long id;
```

```java
    private String title;
    private String author;

    // Constructors
    public Book() {}
    public Book(Long id, String title, String author) {
        this.id = id;
        this.title = title;
        this.author = author;
    }

    // Getters and Setters
    public Long getId() {
        return id;
    }
    public void setId(Long id) {
        this.id = id;
    }
    public String getTitle() {
        return title;
    }
    public void setTitle(String title) {
        this.title = title;
    }
    public String getAuthor() {
        return author;
    }
    public void setAuthor(String author) {
        this.author = author;
    }
}
```

Step 2: Refactor the Controller

Modify the BookController to use a list of Book objects instead of strings:

java
CopyEdit

```java
package com.example.demo;

import org.springframework.web.bind.annotation.*;

import java.util.ArrayList;
import java.util.List;

@RestController
@RequestMapping("/api/books")
public class BookController {

    private final List<Book> books = new ArrayList<>();

    @GetMapping
    public List<Book> getBooks() {
        return books;
    }

    @PostMapping
    public String addBook(@RequestBody Book book) {
        books.add(book);
        return "Book added: " + book.getTitle();
    }

    @GetMapping("/{id}")
    public Book getBookById(@PathVariable Long id) {
        return books.stream()
                .filter(book -> book.getId().equals(id))
```

```
            .findFirst()
            .orElseThrow(() -> new RuntimeException("Book not found"));
    }

    @PutMapping("/{id}")
    public String updateBook(@PathVariable Long id, @RequestBody Book updatedBook) {
        Book book = books.stream()
                .filter(b -> b.getId().equals(id))
                .findFirst()
                .orElseThrow(() -> new RuntimeException("Book not found"));

        book.setTitle(updatedBook.getTitle());
        book.setAuthor(updatedBook.getAuthor());
        return "Book updated: " + book.getTitle();
    }

    @DeleteMapping("/{id}")
    public String deleteBook(@PathVariable Long id) {
        books.removeIf(book -> book.getId().equals(id));
        return "Book deleted with ID: " + id;
    }
}
```

Explanation:

- **@RequestMapping("/api/books")**: Groups all endpoints under /api/books.
- **@PathVariable**: Extracts variables from the URL, such as the book ID.
- **@PutMapping**: Updates a book's details.
- **@DeleteMapping**: Deletes a book by its ID.

Best Practices for REST API Development

1. **Follow RESTful Principles**:
   - Use proper HTTP methods (GET, POST, PUT, DELETE).
   - Return appropriate HTTP status codes (e.g., 200 OK, 404 Not Found).
2. **Validation**:
   - Use @Valid and @NotNull annotations for validating input data.
3. **Error Handling**:
   - Use global exception handling with @ControllerAdvice to return meaningful error messages.
4. **Organize Your Code**:
   - Separate concerns by creating services (@Service) for business logic and repositories (@Repository) for database access.
5. **Use DTOs**:
   - Create Data Transfer Objects (DTOs) to decouple your API from your database models.
6. **Documentation**:
   - Use tools like Swagger (via springdoc-openapi) to generate API documentation.

Next Steps

With this foundation, you've learned to create REST APIs in Spring Boot, handle CRUD operations, and follow best practices. In the next section, we'll explore database integration using Spring Data JPA, allowing your APIs to interact with a real database instead of in-memory data.

Database Integration with Spring Data JPA

Spring Data JPA is a powerful abstraction that simplifies database access in Spring Boot applications. It builds on the Java Persistence API (JPA) and provides an easy-to-use interface for interacting with relational databases. By combining Spring Data JPA with Hibernate (the default JPA provider in Spring Boot), you can perform CRUD operations and more without writing boilerplate SQL.

Setting Up Spring Data JPA

Add Dependencies: Add the required dependencies in your pom.xml file if they're not already included:

xml

CopyEdit

```
<dependencies>
  <dependency>
    <groupId>org.springframework.boot</groupId>
    <artifactId>spring-boot-starter-data-jpa</artifactId>
  </dependency>
  <dependency>
    <groupId>com.h2database</groupId>
    <artifactId>h2</artifactId>
    <scope>runtime</scope>
  </dependency>
</dependencies>
```

- o **Spring Data JPA**: Provides JPA support and integration with Spring Boot.
- o **H2 Database**: An in-memory database for development and testing.

---

1. **Configure Database Connection**: Add the following to your application.properties file to configure H2 as the database:

   properties

   CopyEdit

   ```
   spring.datasource.url=jdbc:h2:mem:testdb
   spring.datasource.driver-class-name=org.h2.Driver
   spring.datasource.username=sa
   spring.datasource.password=
   spring.jpa.database-platform=org.hibernate.dialect.H2Dialect
   spring.h2.console.enabled=true
   ```

2. **Key Points**:
   - The spring.datasource.url specifies the H2 database URL.
   - spring.h2.console.enabled=true enables the H2 web console, accessible at http://localhost:8080/h2-console.

Create a JPA Entity: Define an entity class that maps to a database table. For example:

java

CopyEdit

```
package com.example.demo;

import jakarta.persistence.Entity;
import jakarta.persistence.GeneratedValue;
import jakarta.persistence.GenerationType;
import jakarta.persistence.Id;

@Entity
public class Book {

    @Id
    @GeneratedValue(strategy = GenerationType.IDENTITY)
    private Long id;

    private String title;
    private String author;

    // Constructors
    public Book() {}
    public Book(String title, String author) {
        this.title = title;
        this.author = author;
    }

    // Getters and Setters
```

```java
public Long getId() {
    return id;
}

public void setId(Long id) {
    this.id = id;
}

public String getTitle() {
    return title;
}

public void setTitle(String title) {
    this.title = title;
}

public String getAuthor() {
    return author;
}

public void setAuthor(String author) {
    this.author = author;
}
}
```

3. **Annotations**:
   - @Entity: Marks the class as a JPA entity.
   - @Id: Specifies the primary key.
   - @GeneratedValue: Configures auto-generation of primary key values.

Create a Repository: Spring Data JPA provides a simple interface for database operations. Define a repository interface for the Book entity:

java

```
package com.example.demo;

import org.springframework.data.jpa.repository.JpaRepository;

public interface BookRepository extends JpaRepository<Book, Long> {
}
```

4. **Key Features**:
   - JpaRepository **includes methods like** save, findById, findAll, deleteById, etc.
   - Custom queries can be added if needed.

Write a Service Layer: Use a service class to encapsulate business logic and interact with the repository:

java

```
package com.example.demo;

import org.springframework.stereotype.Service;
import java.util.List;

@Service
public class BookService {

    private final BookRepository bookRepository;

    public BookService(BookRepository bookRepository) {
        this.bookRepository = bookRepository;
    }

    public List<Book> getAllBooks() {
        return bookRepository.findAll();
    }
```

```java
public Book getBookById(Long id) {
    return bookRepository.findById(id).orElseThrow(() -> new RuntimeException("Book not found"));
}

public Book saveBook(Book book) {
    return bookRepository.save(book);
}

public void deleteBook(Long id) {
    bookRepository.deleteById(id);
}
}
```

5. **Update the Controller**: Modify the BookController to use the service layer:
   java
   CopyEdit

```java
package com.example.demo;

import org.springframework.web.bind.annotation.*;
import java.util.List;

@RestController
@RequestMapping("/api/books")
public class BookController {

    private final BookService bookService;

    public BookController(BookService bookService) {
        this.bookService = bookService;
    }
```

```java
@GetMapping
public List<Book> getBooks() {
    return bookService.getAllBooks();
}

@GetMapping("/{id}")
public Book getBookById(@PathVariable Long id) {
    return bookService.getBookById(id);
}

@PostMapping
public Book addBook(@RequestBody Book book) {
    return bookService.saveBook(book);
}

@DeleteMapping("/{id}")
public String deleteBook(@PathVariable Long id) {
    bookService.deleteBook(id);
    return "Book deleted with ID: " + id;
}
}
```

Error Handling and Validation in Spring Boot

Error handling and validation ensure a robust application by preventing bad data and providing meaningful feedback to users. Spring Boot provides built-in tools to handle exceptions and validate inputs.

Validation with Spring Boot

Add Validation Annotations: Use JPA and Bean Validation annotations to enforce constraints on entity fields:

java

CopyEdit

```java
import jakarta.validation.constraints.NotBlank;

@Entity
public class Book {

    @Id
    @GeneratedValue(strategy = GenerationType.IDENTITY)
    private Long id;

    @NotBlank(message = "Title is mandatory")
    private String title;

    @NotBlank(message = "Author is mandatory")
    private String author;

    // Getters and setters...
}
```

1. **Annotations**:
   - **@NotBlank**: Ensures the field is not null or empty.
   - **@Size**: Limits the length of a field.
   - **@Min/@Max**: Sets minimum and maximum numeric values.

Validate Input in the Controller: Use the @Valid annotation in controller methods to validate incoming requests:

java

CopyEdit

```java
@PostMapping
```

```java
public Book addBook(@Valid @RequestBody Book book) {
    return bookService.saveBook(book);
}
```

2. **Note**: If validation fails, Spring automatically returns a 400 Bad Request response with details of the error.

Global Error Handling

Spring Boot provides a way to centralize exception handling using the @ControllerAdvice annotation.

Create a Global Exception Handler:
java
CopyEdit
```java
package com.example.demo;

import org.springframework.http.HttpStatus;
import org.springframework.http.ResponseEntity;
import org.springframework.web.bind.annotation.ControllerAdvice;
import org.springframework.web.bind.annotation.ExceptionHandler;

@ControllerAdvice
public class GlobalExceptionHandler {

    @ExceptionHandler(RuntimeException.class)
    public ResponseEntity<String> handleRuntimeException(RuntimeException ex) {
        return ResponseEntity.status(HttpStatus.BAD_REQUEST).body(ex.getMessage());
    }
}
```

1. **Handle Custom Exceptions**: Create a custom exception class:

java

CopyEdit

```
public class BookNotFoundException extends RuntimeException {

public BookNotFoundException(String message) {
    super(message);
  }
}
```

Modify the service to throw this exception:

java

CopyEdit

```
public Book getBookById(Long id) {
    return bookRepository.findById(id).orElseThrow(() -> new
BookNotFoundException("Book not found with ID: " + id));
  }
```

Update the global exception handler:

java

CopyEdit

```
@ExceptionHandler(BookNotFoundException.class)
public ResponseEntity<String> handleBookNotFoundException(BookNotFoundException
ex) {
    return ResponseEntity.status(HttpStatus.NOT_FOUND).body(ex.getMessage());
  }
```

In this section, you've learned how to integrate a database using Spring Data JPA, perform CRUD operations, validate inputs, and handle errors. These capabilities form the backbone of a robust backend, ensuring your application is reliable and user-friendly.

Next, we'll move on to **Securing Your Application** with Spring Security, where we'll explore authentication, authorization, and best practices for securing REST APIs.

Chapter 5: Securing the Backend

Introduction to Spring Security

Spring Security is a powerful and customizable framework designed to secure Java applications. It provides authentication, authorization, and other essential security features, ensuring your backend is robust and protected from unauthorized access. By integrating seamlessly with Spring Boot, Spring Security simplifies implementing security measures while offering flexibility for complex requirements.

Why Use Spring Security?

1. **Authentication and Authorization**:
   - Verifies the identity of users (authentication) and checks their permissions to access resources (authorization).
2. **Out-of-the-Box Features**:
   - Spring Security includes many prebuilt features like form-based login, Basic Authentication, OAuth2, and JWT support.
3. **Integration with Spring Boot**:
   - With Spring Boot, most security configurations are automatically set up with minimal boilerplate code.
4. **Customizable**:
   - Offers complete control to define custom authentication and authorization logic, tailored to your application's requirements.
5. **Protecting REST APIs**:
   - Prevents unauthorized access to sensitive endpoints and supports token-based authentication methods like OAuth2 and JWT.

Spring Security Basics

Spring Security primarily revolves around two key concepts: **Authentication** and **Authorization**.

1. **Authentication**:
   - Ensures the user is who they claim to be.
   - Common authentication mechanisms include usernames and passwords, OAuth2 tokens, and API keys.
2. **Authorization**:
   - Determines what resources an authenticated user is allowed to access.
   - Resources can include APIs, database records, or files.

Getting Started with Spring Security

Let's secure a Spring Boot application step by step using Spring Security.

Step 1: Add Spring Security to Your Project

Add the following dependency to your pom.xml file:

xml
CopyEdit

```xml
<dependency>
    <groupId>org.springframework.boot</groupId>
    <artifactId>spring-boot-starter-security</artifactId>
</dependency>
```

Step 2: Default Security Configuration

Once the spring-boot-starter-security dependency is added, Spring Boot automatically applies a default security configuration:

1. All endpoints are secured.

2. Basic Authentication is enabled by default.
3. A default username (user) and a randomly generated password are printed in the console when the application starts.

Testing Default Security:

1. Start your application and access any endpoint (e.g., http://localhost:8080/api/books).
2. You'll be prompted to enter a username and password.
3. Use the default credentials:
   - **Username**: user
   - **Password**: Check the console output for the generated password.

Step 3: Customizing Security Configuration

Default behavior is often insufficient for most applications. To customize Spring Security, create a SecurityConfig class:

Create a Configuration Class:
java
CopyEdit

```
package com.example.demo;

import org.springframework.context.annotation.Bean;
import org.springframework.context.annotation.Configuration;
import org.springframework.security.config.annotation.web.builders.HttpSecurity;
import org.springframework.security.web.SecurityFilterChain;

@Configuration
public class SecurityConfig {

    @Bean
    public SecurityFilterChain securityFilterChain(HttpSecurity http) throws Exception {
        http
            .csrf().disable() // Disable CSRF for simplicity (not recommended for production)
```

```
      .authorizeHttpRequests()
         .requestMatchers("/public/**").permitAll() // Allow public endpoints
         .anyRequest().authenticated() // Secure all other endpoints
      .and()
      .httpBasic(); // Enable Basic Authentication
   return http.build();
  }
}
```

1. **Explanation**:
   - ○ **csrf().disable()**: Disables Cross-Site Request Forgery protection (not recommended for production).
   - ○ **authorizeHttpRequests()**: Defines access rules for endpoints.
     - ■ **requestMatchers("/public/**").permitAll**: Allows unrestricted access to paths under /public.
     - ■ **anyRequest().authenticated()**: Requires authentication for all other endpoints.
   - ○ **httpBasic()**: Enables Basic Authentication.
2. **Test the Configuration**:

Create a public endpoint:

java

CopyEdit

```
@RestController
@RequestMapping("/public")
public class PublicController {
  @GetMapping("/welcome")
  public String welcome() {
    return "Welcome to the public endpoint!";
  }
}
```

   - ○
   - ○ **Access** /public/welcome **without authentication—it should work.**

- ○ Access a secured endpoint like /api/books—you'll be prompted for credentials.

Step 4: Customizing User Authentication

By default, Spring Security uses in-memory authentication with a single user. Let's configure custom users for better control.

In-Memory Authentication: Update the SecurityConfig class:

java

CopyEdit

```java
import org.springframework.security.core.userdetails.User;
import org.springframework.security.core.userdetails.UserDetails;
import org.springframework.security.crypto.bcrypt.BCryptPasswordEncoder;
import org.springframework.security.crypto.password.PasswordEncoder;

@Bean
public PasswordEncoder passwordEncoder() {
    return new BCryptPasswordEncoder();
}

@Bean
public UserDetailsService userDetailsService() {
    UserDetails user = User.builder()
        .username("admin")
        .password(passwordEncoder().encode("admin123"))
        .roles("ADMIN")
        .build();

    UserDetails user2 = User.builder()
        .username("user")
        .password(passwordEncoder().encode("user123"))
        .roles("USER")
```

```
        .build();

    return new InMemoryUserDetailsManager(user, user2);
}
```

1. **Explanation**:
   - UserDetailsService: Configures users and their roles.
   - BCryptPasswordEncoder: Encrypts passwords for security.
2. **Test Custom Authentication**:
   - Use the following credentials:
     - **Admin:** admin / admin123
     - **User:** user / user123

Step 5: Role-Based Authorization

Spring Security allows fine-grained control over access based on roles.

Update your SecurityConfig:

java

CopyEdit

```
http
    .authorizeHttpRequests()
        .requestMatchers("/admin/**").hasRole("ADMIN")
        .requestMatchers("/user/**").hasAnyRole("USER", "ADMIN")
        .anyRequest().authenticated()
    .and()
    .httpBasic();
```

1. Create role-specific endpoints:

   java

   CopyEdit

   ```
   @RestController
   @RequestMapping("/admin")
   ```

```java
public class AdminController {
  @GetMapping("/dashboard")
  public String adminDashboard() {
    return "Welcome to the Admin Dashboard!";
  }
}


@RestController
@RequestMapping("/user")
public class UserController {
  @GetMapping("/profile")
  public String userProfile() {
    return "Welcome to the User Profile!";
  }
}
```

2. **Behavior**:
   - /admin/dashboard: **Accessible only by users with the** ADMIN **role.**
   - /user/profile: **Accessible by users with** USER **or** ADMIN **roles.**

Step 6: Securing REST APIs with JWT

JWT (JSON Web Token) is a common mechanism for securing APIs, particularly in stateless applications.

Add JWT Dependency: Add the following dependency:
xml
CopyEdit

```xml
<dependency>
  <groupId>io.jsonwebtoken</groupId>
  <artifactId>jjwt-api</artifactId>
  <version>0.11.5</version>
</dependency>
```

1. **Generate JWTs**: Create a utility class for generating tokens:
   java
   CopyEdit

```java
import io.jsonwebtoken.Jwts;

import io.jsonwebtoken.SignatureAlgorithm;

import java.util.Date;

public class JwtUtil {
    private static final String SECRET_KEY = "mySecretKey";

    public static String generateToken(String username) {
        return Jwts.builder()
            .setSubject(username)
            .setIssuedAt(new Date())
            .setExpiration(new Date(System.currentTimeMillis() + 1000 * 60 * 60 * 10)) // 10 hours
            .signWith(SignatureAlgorithm.HS256, SECRET_KEY)
            .compact();
    }
}
```

2. **Validate JWTs**: Implement a filter to verify JWTs for secured endpoints (e.g., using OncePerRequestFilter).

Spring Security provides powerful tools to secure your backend, from simple in-memory authentication to advanced role-based access and JWT-based token authentication. In this chapter, you learned how to configure security for your Spring Boot application, including role-based authorization and securing REST APIs.

JWT Authentication and Authorization

JSON Web Token (JWT) is a widely used standard for securing REST APIs. It allows servers to authenticate and authorize users by issuing digitally signed tokens that clients include in their requests. These tokens eliminate the need for servers to maintain session state, making JWTs particularly useful in stateless, scalable applications.

What is JWT?

A JWT is a compact, URL-safe token that encodes information about the user and their permissions. It consists of three parts:

Header: Specifies the token type (JWT) and signing algorithm (e.g., HMAC SHA256). Example:
json
CopyEdit

```json
{

  "alg": "HS256",

  "typ": "JWT"

}
```

1.

Payload: Contains claims (information about the user or application). Example:
json
CopyEdit

```json
{

  "sub": "user@example.com",

  "role": "USER",

  "exp": 1675270200
```

}

2.

3. **Signature**: Verifies the token's integrity using a secret key or private key.

The final token is a Base64-encoded string in this format:

php

CopyEdit

<Header>.<Payload>.<Signature>

Step 1: Add JWT Dependencies

Add the following dependencies to your pom.xml file:

xml

CopyEdit

```
<dependency>

    <groupId>io.jsonwebtoken</groupId>

    <artifactId>jjwt-api</artifactId>

    <version>0.11.5</version>

</dependency>

<dependency>

    <groupId>io.jsonwebtoken</groupId>

    <artifactId>jjwt-impl</artifactId>

    <version>0.11.5</version>
```

63

```
    <scope>runtime</scope>

</dependency>

<dependency>

    <groupId>io.jsonwebtoken</groupId>

    <artifactId>jjwt-jackson</artifactId>

    <version>0.11.5</version>

    <scope>runtime</scope>

</dependency>
```

Step 2: Create a JWT Utility Class

Create a utility class to generate and validate JWTs:

java

CopyEdit

```java
package com.example.demo.security;


import io.jsonwebtoken.Claims;

import io.jsonwebtoken.Jwts;

import io.jsonwebtoken.SignatureAlgorithm;


import org.springframework.stereotype.Component;
```

```java
import java.util.Date;

@Component
public class JwtUtil {

    private static final String SECRET_KEY = "mySecretKey";
    private static final long EXPIRATION_TIME = 1000 * 60 * 60 * 10; // 10 hours

    public String generateToken(String username) {
        return Jwts.builder()
            .setSubject(username)
            .setIssuedAt(new Date())
            .setExpiration(new Date(System.currentTimeMillis() + EXPIRATION_TIME))
            .signWith(SignatureAlgorithm.HS256, SECRET_KEY)
            .compact();
    }

    public String extractUsername(String token) {
        return getClaims(token).getSubject();
    }
```

```java
public boolean validateToken(String token, String username) {

    return username.equals(extractUsername(token)) && !isTokenExpired(token);

}


private boolean isTokenExpired(String token) {

    return getClaims(token).getExpiration().before(new Date());

}


private Claims getClaims(String token) {

    return Jwts.parser()

        .setSigningKey(SECRET_KEY)

        .parseClaimsJws(token)

        .getBody();

    }

}
```

Step 3: Implement Authentication

Create a Login Endpoint: Create a controller for user authentication:
java

```java
@RestController

@RequestMapping("/auth")

public class AuthController {


    private final JwtUtil jwtUtil;


    public AuthController(JwtUtil jwtUtil) {

        this.jwtUtil = jwtUtil;

    }


    @PostMapping("/login")

    public ResponseEntity<String> login(@RequestBody AuthRequest authRequest) {

        // For demonstration, assume authentication is successful

        String token = jwtUtil.generateToken(authRequest.getUsername());

        return ResponseEntity.ok(token);

    }

}


class AuthRequest {

    private String username;

    private String password;
```

```
// Getters and Setters

}
```

1. **Secure Endpoints with JWT**: Create a filter to validate tokens for secured endpoints:
   java
   CopyEdit

```java
import org.springframework.security.core.context.SecurityContextHolder;

import org.springframework.web.filter.OncePerRequestFilter;


import javax.servlet.FilterChain;

import javax.servlet.ServletException;

import javax.servlet.http.HttpServletRequest;

import javax.servlet.http.HttpServletResponse;

import java.io.IOException;


public class JwtFilter extends OncePerRequestFilter {


    private final JwtUtil jwtUtil;


    public JwtFilter(JwtUtil jwtUtil) {

        this.jwtUtil = jwtUtil;

    }
```

```java
@Override

protected void doFilterInternal(HttpServletRequest request, HttpServletResponse response,
FilterChain filterChain) throws ServletException, IOException {

    String authorizationHeader = request.getHeader("Authorization");


    if (authorizationHeader != null && authorizationHeader.startsWith("Bearer ")) {

        String token = authorizationHeader.substring(7);

        String username = jwtUtil.extractUsername(token);


        if (jwtUtil.validateToken(token, username)) {

            SecurityContextHolder.getContext().setAuthentication(new
JwtAuthenticationToken(username));

        }
    }


    filterChain.doFilter(request, response);

    }

}
```

Step 4: Test the JWT Flow

Login to Generate a Token: Send a POST request to /auth/login with the username and
password:
json

CopyEdit

```json
{
  "username": "user",
  "password": "password"
}
```

Response:
json
CopyEdit

```json
{
  "token": "eyJhbGciOiJIUzI1NiIsInR5cCI6IkpXVCJ9..."
}
```

Access Secured Endpoints: Include the token in the Authorization header:
makefile
CopyEdit

```
Authorization: Bearer <token>
```

Implementing OAuth2 for Social Logins

OAuth2 is an open standard for access delegation, commonly used to enable social logins (e.g., Google, Facebook). Spring Security simplifies OAuth2 integration for social logins.

Step 1: Add OAuth2 Dependencies

Add the following dependencies to your pom.xml:

xml

CopyEdit

```
<dependency>
    <groupId>org.springframework.boot</groupId>
    <artifactId>spring-boot-starter-oauth2-client</artifactId>
</dependency>
```

Step 2: Configure OAuth2 Login

Update application.properties: Add configuration for Google login:

properties

CopyEdit

```
spring.security.oauth2.client.registration.google.client-id=your-client-id

spring.security.oauth2.client.registration.google.client-secret=your-client-secret

spring.security.oauth2.client.registration.google.scope=openid,profile,email

spring.security.oauth2.client.provider.google.authorization-uri=https://accounts.google.com/o/oauth2/v2/auth

spring.security.oauth2.client.provider.google.token-uri=https://oauth2.googleapis.com/token

spring.security.oauth2.client.provider.google.user-info-uri=https://www.googleapis.com/oauth2/v3/userinfo
```

Enable OAuth2 Login: Update the SecurityConfig:

java

CopyEdit

```
http

    .authorizeHttpRequests()

        .anyRequest().authenticated()

    .and()

    .oauth2Login();
```

Step 3: Test the OAuth2 Flow

1. Access the application in your browser. You'll be redirected to Google's login page.
2. After successful login, you'll be redirected back to your application with user details.

In this section, you've implemented JWT-based authentication and configured OAuth2 for social logins. JWTs provide a stateless way to secure APIs, while OAuth2 enables seamless integration with external identity providers like Google. These techniques ensure robust, scalable, and user-friendly security for your backend.

Next, we'll explore **Building the Frontend with React**, where we'll integrate these security mechanisms into a dynamic user interface.

Chapter 6: React Fundamentals

Understanding React Components, Props, and State

React is a JavaScript library for building user interfaces, and at its core are **components**, **props**, and **state**. These foundational concepts allow you to build interactive, reusable, and dynamic web applications. In this chapter, we'll break down each concept, explain how they work, and demonstrate how to use them effectively.

What Are React Components?

A **component** in React is a reusable piece of UI. It can be thought of as a JavaScript function or class that outputs HTML elements. React applications are built by combining these components to form a complete user interface.

Types of Components

1. **Functional Components**:
   - These are plain JavaScript functions that return JSX (JavaScript XML).
   - They are the most common type of component in modern React development, especially after the introduction of Hooks.

Example:
javascript
CopyEdit
```javascript
const Welcome = () => {
   return <h1>Welcome to React!</h1>;
};
```

2. **Class Components**:
   - These are ES6 classes that extend React.Component.
   - While still supported, they are less commonly used today due to the rise of functional components and Hooks.

Example:
javascript
CopyEdit
```
class Welcome extends React.Component {
  render() {
    return <h1>Welcome to React!</h1>;
  }
}
```

o

JSX: The Building Block of React

React components use **JSX** to define their UI. JSX is a syntax extension that allows you to write HTML-like code in JavaScript.

Example of JSX:
javascript
CopyEdit
```
const App = () => {
  return (
    <div>
      <h1>Hello, World!</h1>
      <p>This is a React application.</p>
    </div>
  );
};
```

Key Notes on JSX:

- JSX must have a single parent element. For example, wrap elements in a <div> or React fragment (<> </>).
- You can use curly braces ({ }) to embed JavaScript expressions.

Props: Passing Data Between Components

Props (short for "properties") are used to pass data from a parent component to a child component. Props are **read-only** and cannot be modified by the child component.

How Props Work

1. Props are passed to child components as attributes in JSX.
2. They are accessible in the child component via the props object.

Example of Props

Parent Component:

javascript

CopyEdit

```
const App = () => {
  return <Greeting name="John" />;
};
```

1. **Child Component**:

   javascript

   CopyEdit

   ```
   const Greeting = (props) => {
   ```

   ```
     return <h1>Hello, {props.name}!</h1>;
   };
   ```

2. **Output**:

   CopyEdit

   ```
   Hello, John!
   ```

3. **Destructuring Props**

To make the code cleaner, you can destructure props:

javascript

CopyEdit

```
const Greeting = ({ name }) => {
  return <h1>Hello, {name}!</h1>;
```

```
};
```

Passing Multiple Props

You can pass multiple props to a component:

```javascript
CopyEdit
const Profile = ({ name, age }) => {
  return (
    <div>
      <h2>Name: {name}</h2>
      <p>Age: {age}</p>
    </div>
  );
};

const App = () => {
  return <Profile name="Alice" age={30} />;
};
```

State: Managing Dynamic Data

While props are used for passing static data, **state** is used to manage dynamic data that can change over time. State is local to a component and can only be updated within that component.

State in Functional Components

Functional components use the useState **Hook** to manage state.

Import useState:

javascript

CopyEdit

```
import React, { useState } from 'react';
```

1.

Initialize State:

javascript

CopyEdit

```
const Counter = () => {
  const [count, setCount] = useState(0);

  return (
    <div>
      <h1>Count: {count}</h1>
      <button onClick={() => setCount(count + 1)}>Increment</button>
    </div>
  );
};
```

2. **Explanation:**
   - useState(0): Initializes the count variable with a value of 0.
   - setCount: A function to update the state.
   - When the button is clicked, the setCount function updates the state, and the UI re-renders with the new value.

State in Class Components

In class components, state is managed using the state object and updated with the setState method.

Define State:

javascript

CopyEdit

```
class Counter extends React.Component {
```

77

```
constructor() {
  super();
  this.state = { count: 0 };
}

increment = () => {
  this.setState({ count: this.state.count + 1 });
};

render() {
  return (
    <div>
      <h1>Count: {this.state.count}</h1>
      <button onClick={this.increment}>Increment</button>
    </div>
  );
}
}
```

1. **Key Differences**:
   o Functional components use useState, while class components use state and setState.
   o Functional components are preferred in modern React development.

Combining Props and State

Props and state can work together to create dynamic components.

Example: A Simple To-Do List

Parent Component:

javascript

CopyEdit

```
const App = () => {
```

```
const [tasks, setTasks] = useState(["Task 1", "Task 2"]);

const addTask = () => {
  setTasks([...tasks, `Task ${tasks.length + 1}`]);
};

return (
  <div>
    <TaskList tasks={tasks} />
    <button onClick={addTask}>Add Task</button>
  </div>
);
};
```

1. **Child Component**:
   javascript
   CopyEdit
   ```
   const TaskList = ({ tasks }) => {

   return (
     <ul>
       {tasks.map((task, index) => (
         <li key={index}>{task}</li>
       ))}
     </ul>
   );
   };
   ```

2. **Explanation**:
   - The App component manages the state (tasks).
   - The TaskList component receives tasks as a prop and renders the list.

Best Practices for Components, Props, and State

1. **Keep Components Small and Focused**:
   - Each component should handle a single responsibility.
   - If a component grows too large, break it into smaller components.

2. **Avoid Mutating State Directly**:
   - Always use setState or the updater function from useState to update state.

Example (incorrect):

javascript

CopyEdit

this.state.count = 1; // Do not do this

   -

3. **Pass Only Necessary Props**:
   - Avoid passing unnecessary props to child components to keep your code clean and efficient.

4. **Use Keys for Lists**:
   - When rendering lists, always include a unique key prop to help React identify items and optimize rendering.

React components, props, and state form the backbone of any React application. Components allow you to break your UI into reusable pieces, props enable you to pass data between these pieces, and state provides dynamic behavior. With these tools, you can build powerful and interactive user interfaces.

In the next chapter, we'll explore **State Management in React**, diving deeper into advanced state management techniques using Context API and Redux Toolkit.

React Hooks: useState, useEffect, and Beyond

React Hooks are functions that allow functional components to manage state and side effects. Introduced in React 16.8, Hooks revolutionized how React applications are built by enabling the use of state and lifecycle features in functional components, eliminating the need for class components.

What Are Hooks?

Hooks are special functions that let you "hook into" React's features. They enable you to manage state, perform side effects, and leverage advanced React capabilities, all within functional components.

Rules of Hooks

1. **Call Hooks at the Top Level**: Don't call Hooks inside loops, conditions, or nested functions.
2. **Call Hooks Only in React Functions**: Use them in functional components or custom Hooks, not in regular JavaScript functions.

---

useState: Managing State

useState is the most commonly used Hook for managing state in functional components. It allows you to add local state to a component.

Basic Usage

javascript

CopyEdit

```javascript
import React, { useState } from "react";


const Counter = () => {

  const [count, setCount] = useState(0); // Initialize state with 0
```

```javascript
const increment = () => {

  setCount(count + 1); // Update state

};


return (

  <div>

    <h1>Count: {count}</h1>

    <button onClick={increment}>Increment</button>

  </div>

);

};
```

Explanation:

- **useState(0)**: Initializes the count variable with 0.
- **setCount**: A function to update the state.

Managing Complex State

You can use useState to manage objects or arrays:

javascript

CopyEdit

```javascript
const UserProfile = () => {

  const [user, setUser] = useState({ name: "Alice", age: 25 });
```

```javascript
const updateName = () => {

  setUser({ ...user, name: "Bob" }); // Use spread operator to retain other properties

};


return (

  <div>

    <h2>Name: {user.name}</h2>

    <h3>Age: {user.age}</h3>

    <button onClick={updateName}>Update Name</button>

  </div>

);

};
```

---

useEffect: Managing Side Effects

useEffect is used to perform side effects in functional components, such as fetching data, updating the DOM, or subscribing to events. It replaces lifecycle methods like componentDidMount, componentDidUpdate, and componentWillUnmount in class components.

Basic Usage

javascript

CopyEdit

```jsx
import React, { useState, useEffect } from "react";


const Timer = () => {

  const [seconds, setSeconds] = useState(0);


  useEffect(() => {

    const interval = setInterval(() => {

      setSeconds((prev) => prev + 1);

    }, 1000);


    return () => clearInterval(interval); // Cleanup to avoid memory leaks

  }, []); // Empty dependency array: runs only once when the component mounts


  return <h1>Seconds: {seconds}</h1>;

};
```

Key Points:

- **Dependencies**: The second argument to useEffect is an array of dependencies that determine when the effect runs.
    - []: Runs the effect only once when the component mounts.
    - [someVariable]: Runs the effect whenever someVariable changes.
    - Omit the array to run the effect after every render.

Advanced Hooks

1. **useContext**:
   - Allows components to consume context data without passing props down manually.
   - Useful for global state management.

javascript
CopyEdit

```
const ThemeContext = React.createContext("light");


const App = () => {

  return (

    <ThemeContext.Provider value="dark">

      <Toolbar />

    </ThemeContext.Provider>

  );

};


const Toolbar = () => {

  const theme = React.useContext(ThemeContext);

  return <h1>Current Theme: {theme}</h1>;

};
```

2. **useReducer**:
   - A more advanced alternative to useState for managing complex state logic.

```javascript
CopyEdit
const reducer = (state, action) => {

    switch (action.type) {

      case "increment":

        return { count: state.count + 1 };

      case "decrement":

        return { count: state.count - 1 };

      default:

        return state;

    }

};


const Counter = () => {

    const [state, dispatch] = useReducer(reducer, { count: 0 });


    return (

      <div>

        <h1>Count: {state.count}</h1>

        <button onClick={() => dispatch({ type: "increment" })}>+</button>

        <button onClick={() => dispatch({ type: "decrement" })}>-</button>

      </div>
```

```
  );
};
```

3. Custom Hooks:
- o Create reusable logic by writing your own Hooks.

javascript
CopyEdit

```javascript
const useWindowWidth = () => {

  const [width, setWidth] = useState(window.innerWidth);


  useEffect(() => {

    const handleResize = () => setWidth(window.innerWidth);

    window.addEventListener("resize", handleResize);

    return () => window.removeEventListener("resize", handleResize);

  }, []);


  return width;

};


const App = () => {

  const width = useWindowWidth();

  return <h1>Window Width: {width}</h1>;

};
```

Building Your First React Application

Let's build a simple React application step-by-step to reinforce these concepts.

Step 1: Set Up Your Project

Install Node.js:
Ensure Node.js is installed by running:
bash
CopyEdit

```
node -v

npm -v
```

1. **Create a React App**:
   Use Create React App to set up a new project:
   bash
   CopyEdit

   ```
   npx create-react-app my-first-app

   cd my-first-app

   npm start
   ```

2. **Start the Development Server**:
   The app will open in your browser at http://localhost:3000.

Step 2: Create Components

App.js:
Modify the default App.js file to include a header and a placeholder for tasks:
javascript
CopyEdit

```
import React from "react";
```

```javascript
import TaskManager from "./TaskManager";

const App = () => {
  return (
    <div>
      <h1>Task Manager</h1>
      <TaskManager />
    </div>
  );
};

export default App;
```

1. **TaskManager Component**:
   Create a new file TaskManager.js:
   javascript
   CopyEdit

```javascript
import React, { useState } from "react";

const TaskManager = () => {
  const [tasks, setTasks] = useState([]);
  const [task, setTask] = useState("");

  const addTask = () => {
```

```jsx
    if (task.trim()) {

      setTasks([...tasks, task]);

      setTask("");

    }

  };


  return (

    <div>

      <input

        type="text"

        value={task}

        onChange={(e) => setTask(e.target.value)}

        placeholder="Add a new task"

      />

      <button onClick={addTask}>Add Task</button>

      <ul>

        {tasks.map((t, index) => (

          <li key={index}>{t}</li>

        ))}

      </ul>

    </div>
```

```
      );

  };


export default TaskManager;
```

Step 3: Test the Application

Run the app and interact with the Task Manager:

- Add new tasks using the input field.
- View the dynamically updated list.

Enhancements

1. **Use Local Storage**:
   Persist tasks across browser sessions using useEffect and localStorage.
2. **Delete Tasks**:
   Add a delete button next to each task to remove it.
3. **Styling**:
   Use CSS or a library like TailwindCSS to improve the UI.

This chapter introduced React Hooks like useState, useEffect, and advanced Hooks, along with building a functional application. These concepts are the foundation of modern React development. In the next chapter, we'll explore **State Management in React**, focusing on Context API and Redux Toolkit.

Chapter 7: Building the Frontend with React

Styling Applications with TailwindCSS, Material-UI, and CSS

Styling plays a critical role in making your React applications visually appealing and user-friendly. React offers flexibility in how you approach styling, whether it's using plain CSS, utility-first frameworks like TailwindCSS, or component-based libraries like Material-UI. In this chapter, we'll explore these three approaches and demonstrate how to style a React application effectively.

Plain CSS: The Foundation of Styling

CSS (Cascading Style Sheets) is the most basic way to style a React application. React allows you to use global CSS files or modular CSS for scoping styles to individual components.

Global CSS

1. **Adding a Global CSS File**:
    - Create a styles.css file in the src folder.

Add the following styles:
css
CopyEdit
```css
body {
    font-family: Arial, sans-serif;
    margin: 0;
    padding: 0;
    background-color: #f5f5f5;
}

h1 {
    color: #333;
    text-align: center;
```

}

2. **Import the CSS File**:

Import the styles.css file into your index.js or App.js file:

javascript

CopyEdit

```
import "./styles.css";
```

Example Usage:

javascript

CopyEdit

```
const Header = () => {
  return <h1>Welcome to My React App</h1>;
};

export default Header;
```

3. **CSS Modules**

CSS Modules allow you to scope CSS styles to specific components, preventing style conflicts.

1. **Create a CSS Module File**:

Create Header.module.css:

css

CopyEdit

```
header {
  color: #fff;
  background-color: #007bff;
  padding: 10px;
  text-align: center;
  border-radius: 5px;
}
```

○

Use the CSS Module in a Component:

javascript

CopyEdit

```javascript
import styles from "./Header.module.css";

const Header = () => {
  return <h1 className={styles.header}>Welcome to My React App</h1>;
};

export default Header;
```

2. **Benefits of CSS Modules**:

- Styles are scoped to components by default.
- Prevents naming conflicts in large applications.

TailwindCSS: A Utility-First Framework

TailwindCSS is a popular CSS framework that provides utility classes for styling elements directly in your HTML or JSX. It eliminates the need for custom CSS by offering pre-designed utility classes.

Setting Up TailwindCSS

Install TailwindCSS: Run the following commands to install TailwindCSS:

bash

CopyEdit

```bash
npm install -D tailwindcss postcss autoprefixer
npx tailwindcss init
```

1. **Configure Tailwind**: Add the paths to your React components in the content array of tailwind.config.js:

   javascript

   CopyEdit

   ```javascript
   module.exports = {
   ```

```
  content: [
    "./src/**/*.{js,jsx,ts,tsx}",
  ].
  theme: {
    extend: {},
  },
  plugins: [],
};
```

2. **Add Tailwind to CSS**: Update your index.css or styles.css:

   css

   CopyEdit

   @tailwind base;

@tailwind components;
@tailwind utilities;

3. **Start the Development Server**: TailwindCSS is now ready to use. Restart your development server:

   bash

   CopyEdit

   npm start

4. **Using TailwindCSS in Components**

Example Header Component:

javascript

CopyEdit

```javascript
const Header = () => {
  return (
    <header className="bg-blue-500 text-white text-center p-4 rounded-md">
      <h1 className="text-2xl font-bold">Welcome to My React App</h1>
    </header>
  );
};
```

export default Header;

1. **Key Benefits**:
   - Rapid development with utility classes.
   - Consistent, responsive designs with minimal effort.
   - Highly customizable via the tailwind.config.js file.

Material-UI (MUI): A Component-Based Library

Material-UI, now known as MUI, is a popular React component library based on Google's Material Design principles. It provides pre-styled components like buttons, cards, grids, and more.

Setting Up MUI

Install MUI: Install the core library and icons:

bash

CopyEdit

```
npm install @mui/material @emotion/react @emotion/styled
npm install @mui/icons-material
```

1. **Example Usage**: Create a simple button using MUI:

   javascript

   CopyEdit

   ```
   import React from "react";

   import Button from "@mui/material/Button";

   const App = () => {
     return (
       <div style={{ textAlign: "center", marginTop: "20px" }}>
         <Button variant="contained" color="primary">
           Click Me
         </Button>
       </div>
     );
   ```

96

```
};
```

export default App;

2. Customizing MUI Components

You can customize MUI components using its sx prop or theme configuration.

Using the sx Prop:

javascript

CopyEdit

```
import React from "react";
import Button from "@mui/material/Button";

const App = () => {
  return (
    <Button
      variant="contained"
      sx={{
        backgroundColor: "green",
        "&:hover": {
          backgroundColor: "darkgreen",
        },
      }}
    >
      Custom Button
    </Button>
  );
};

export default App;
```

1. **Customizing the Theme**:
   javascript
   CopyEdit

```javascript
import React from "react";

import { createTheme, ThemeProvider } from "@mui/material/styles";
import Button from "@mui/material/Button";

const theme = createTheme({
  palette: {
    primary: {
      main: "#ff5722",
    },
  },
});

const App = () => {
  return (
    <ThemeProvider theme={theme}>
      <Button variant="contained" color="primary">
        Themed Button
      </Button>
    </ThemeProvider>
  );
};

export default App;
```

2. **Advantages of MUI**:

- Ready-to-use, well-designed components.
- Easy customization with themes and the sx prop.
- Extensive documentation and community support.

Comparison of Styling Approaches

Feature	Plain CSS	TailwindCSS	Material-UI (MUI)
Ease of Use	Simple but manual	Rapid development	Prebuilt components
Customizability	High	High	High
Scalability	Moderate	Excellent	Excellent
Learning Curve	Low	Moderate	Moderate

Building a Sample Application

Let's build a simple "Profile Card" component using each approach to see how they compare.

1. Plain CSS

css

CopyEdit

```css
/* ProfileCard.module.css */
.card {
    background-color: white;
    padding: 20px;
    border-radius: 10px;
    box-shadow: 0 4px 6px rgba(0, 0, 0, 0.1);
    text-align: center;
}
```

javascript

CopyEdit

```javascript
import styles from "./ProfileCard.module.css";

const ProfileCard = () => {
    return (
        <div className={styles.card}>
            <h2>John Doe</h2>
            <p>Software Engineer</p>
```

```
    </div>
  );
};


export default ProfileCard;
```

---

2. TailwindCSS

javascript

CopyEdit

```
const ProfileCard = () => {
  return (
    <div className="bg-white p--4 rounded-lg shadow-md text-center">
      <h2 className="text-xl font-bold">John Doe</h2>
      <p className="text-gray-500">Software Engineer</p>
    </div>
  );
};


export default ProfileCard;
```

---

3. Material-UI

javascript

CopyEdit

```
import React from "react";
import Card from "@mui/material/Card";
import CardContent from "@mui/material/CardContent";
import Typography from "@mui/material/Typography";

const ProfileCard = () => {
  return (
```

```
<Card sx={{ maxWidth: 300, margin: "0 auto", textAlign: "center" }}>
  <CardContent>
    <Typography variant="h5" component="div">
    John Doe
    </Typography>
    <Typography color="text.secondary">Software Engineer</Typography>
  </CardContent>
</Card>
);
};

export default ProfileCard;
```

Styling React applications can range from using plain CSS for simplicity to leveraging advanced tools like TailwindCSS and Material-UI for rapid and professional-grade designs. Each approach has its strengths, and your choice depends on the project requirements, team preferences, and the complexity of your application.

In the next chapter, we'll explore **State Management in React**, focusing on how to handle global and shared state using the Context API and Redux Toolkit.

State Management with Context API and Redux Toolkit

Managing state is a core part of any React application, especially when dealing with shared or global state. React provides several ways to handle state, with the **Context API** and **Redux Toolkit** being two powerful tools for managing state across components.

What Is State Management?

State management is the process of storing and updating the data (state) that your application uses to function. In simple apps, local state (managed with useState) is sufficient. However,

101

in larger applications, where data needs to be shared across multiple components, a centralized state management solution is often required.

Context API

The **Context API** is a built-in feature in React that provides a way to share data across the component tree without manually passing props at every level. It's ideal for small to medium-scale applications.

When to Use Context API

- Sharing data like themes, user authentication, or localization.
- Avoiding "prop drilling" (passing props down multiple levels).

How Context API Works

Create a Context: Use React.createContext() to create a context object.
javascript
CopyEdit

```javascript
import React, { createContext, useState, useContext } from "react";

const ThemeContext = createContext();
```

1. **Provide the Context**: Wrap the components that need access to the context with a Provider and pass the shared state.
   javascript
   CopyEdit

   ```javascript
   const ThemeProvider = ({ children }) => {

   const [theme, setTheme] = useState("light");

   return (
     <ThemeContext.Provider value={{ theme, setTheme }}>
       {children}
   ```

```
    </ThemeContext.Provider>
  );
};
```

export default ThemeProvider;

2. **Consume the Context**: Use useContext to access the context data in any child
   component.
   javascript
   CopyEdit
   ```
   const ThemeSwitcher = () => {

   const { theme, setTheme } = useContext(ThemeContext);

   return (
     <div>
       <p>Current Theme: {theme}</p>
       <button onClick={() => setTheme(theme === "light" ? "dark" : "light")}>
         Toggle Theme
       </button>
     </div>
   );
};
   ```

3. **Integrate the Provider**: Wrap your application with the ThemeProvider in App.js:
   javascript
   CopyEdit
   ```
   import ThemeProvider from "./ThemeProvider";

   const App = () => {
     return (
       <ThemeProvider>
         <ThemeSwitcher />
       </ThemeProvider>
   ```

103

```
  );
};
```

export default App;

4. Redux Toolkit

Redux is a powerful library for managing global state, especially in complex applications. Redux Toolkit (RTK) simplifies Redux by providing tools for efficient state management and reducing boilerplate code.

When to Use Redux Toolkit

- When your application has complex state logic or requires middleware for tasks like API calls.
- When multiple components need access to shared state that changes frequently.

Setting Up Redux Toolkit

Install Redux Toolkit:

bash

CopyEdit

```
npm install @reduxjs/toolkit react-redux
```

1. **Create a Redux Slice**: A "slice" is a collection of state and reducers.

   javascript

   CopyEdit

   ```
   import { createSlice } from "@reduxjs/toolkit";
   ```

```javascript
const counterSlice = createSlice({
  name: "counter",
  initialState: { value: 0 },
  reducers: {
    increment: (state) => {
      state.value += 1;
```

```
  },
  decrement: (state) => {
    state.value -= 1;
  },
  incrementByAmount: (state, action) => {
    state.value += action.payload;
  },
},
});

export const { increment, decrement, incrementByAmount } = counterSlice.actions;
export default counterSlice.reducer;
```

2. **Configure the Store**: Add the slice reducer to the Redux store.
   javascript
   CopyEdit

```
import { configureStore } from "@reduxjs/toolkit";

import counterReducer from "./counterSlice";

const store = configureStore({
  reducer: {
    counter: counterReducer,
  },
});

export default store;
```

3. **Provide the Store**: Wrap your application with the Redux Provider in index.js:
   javascript
   CopyEdit

```
import React from "react";

import ReactDOM from "react-dom";
import { Provider } from "react-redux";
```

```
import store from "./store";
import App from "./App";

ReactDOM.render(
  <Provider store={store}>
    <App />
  </Provider>,
  document.getElementById("root")
);
```

4. **Use Redux State in Components**: Use the useSelector and useDispatch Hooks to interact with Redux state.
   javascript
   CopyEdit

```
import React from "react";
import { useSelector, useDispatch } from "react-redux";
import { increment, decrement, incrementByAmount } from "./counterSlice";

const Counter = () => {
  const count = useSelector((state) => state.counter.value);
  const dispatch = useDispatch();

  return (
    <div>
      <h1>Count: {count}</h1>
      <button onClick={() => dispatch(increment())}>Increment</button>
      <button onClick={() => dispatch(decrement())}>Decrement</button>
      <button onClick={() => dispatch(incrementByAmount(5))}>
        Increment by 5
      </button>
    </div>
  );
};
```

export default Counter;

Routing and Navigation with React Router

Routing is an essential feature in modern web applications, enabling users to navigate between different pages or views. React Router is the most widely used library for routing in React applications.

Setting Up React Router
Install React Router:
bash
CopyEdit
npm install react-router-dom

1. **Basic Routing Setup**:
   javascript
   CopyEdit
   ```
   import React from "react";

   import { BrowserRouter as Router, Route, Routes } from "react-router-dom";

   const Home = () => <h1>Home Page</h1>;
   const About = () => <h1>About Page</h1>;

   const App = () => {
     return (
       <Router>
         <Routes>
           <Route path="/" element={<Home />} />
           <Route path="/about" element={<About />} />
         </Routes>
       </Router>
   ```

```
  );
};
```

```
export default App;
```

2. **Key Components**:
   - ○ **<Router>**: Wraps your application and enables routing.
   - ○ **<Routes>**: Contains all your route definitions.
   - ○ **<Route>**: Defines a route with a path and an associated component.

Adding Navigation

Using the Link Component:

javascript

CopyEdit

```
import { Link } from "react-router-dom";

const Navbar = () => {
  return (
    <nav>
      <Link to="/">Home</Link>
      <Link to="/about">About</Link>
    </nav>
  );
};
```

1. **Example App with Navigation**:

   javascript

   CopyEdit

   ```
   import React from "react";

   import { BrowserRouter as Router, Route, Routes, Link } from "react-router-dom";

   const Home = () => <h1>Home Page</h1>;
   const About = () => <h1>About Page</h1>;
   ```

```javascript
const App = () => {
  return (
    <Router>
      <nav>
        <Link to="/">Home</Link>
        <Link to="/about">About</Link>
      </nav>
      <Routes>
        <Route path="/" element={<Home />} />
        <Route path="/about" element={<About />} />
      </Routes>
    </Router>
  );
};

export default App;
```

2. Dynamic Routing

Dynamic routing allows you to create routes with parameters.

Define a Route with a Parameter:

javascript

CopyEdit

```javascript
const Profile = ({ id }) => <h1>Profile of User {id}</h1>;

const App = () => {
  return (
    <Router>
      <Routes>
        <Route path="/profile/:id" element={<Profile />} />
      </Routes>
    </Router>
  );
```

109

```
};
```

1. **Access Route Parameters**: Use the useParams Hook:

javascript

CopyEdit

```javascript
import { useParams } from "react-router-dom";


const Profile = () => {
  const { id } = useParams();
  return <h1>Profile of User {id}</h1>;
};
```

2. **Nested Routes**

React Router supports nested routes for more complex applications.

javascript

CopyEdit

```javascript
const Dashboard = () => {
  return (
    <div>
      <h1>Dashboard</h1>
      <Routes>
        <Route path="analytics" element={<h2>Analytics</h2>} />
        <Route path="settings" element={<h2>Settings</h2>} />
      </Routes>
    </div>
  );
};


const App = () => {
  return (
    <Router>
      <Routes>
        <Route path="/dashboard/*" element={<Dashboard />} />
```

```
      </Routes>
     </Router>
   );
};
```

State management with Context API and Redux Toolkit provides the tools to handle complex, shared application state effectively, while React Router simplifies navigation and routing in React applications. Together, they form the backbone of scalable, user-friendly React projects.

In the next chapter, we'll focus on **Connecting React to Spring Boot**, bridging the gap between the frontend and backend for seamless full-stack development.

Chapter 8: Integrating Frontend and Backend

Setting Up API Communication Between React and Spring Boot

Connecting the frontend (React) and backend (Spring Boot) is essential for building dynamic, full-stack applications. This chapter will guide you through the process of setting up seamless communication between the two using REST APIs.

Understanding the Workflow

1. **Frontend (React)**:
   - Sends HTTP requests (e.g., GET, POST) to the backend via REST API endpoints.
   - Receives data (usually in JSON format) from the backend.
2. **Backend (Spring Boot)**:
   - Processes requests from the frontend.
   - Retrieves or updates data in the database.
   - Sends a response back to the frontend.

Step 1: Setting Up the Backend (Spring Boot)

Ensure your Spring Boot application is ready with REST API endpoints.

Example: Building a Simple REST API
Create a REST Controller:
java
CopyEdit

```
package com.example.demo;

import org.springframework.web.bind.annotation.*;

import java.util.ArrayList;
```

```java
import java.util.List;

@RestController
@RequestMapping("/api/tasks")
public class TaskController {

    private final List<Task> tasks = new ArrayList<>();

    @GetMapping
    public List<Task> getTasks() {
        return tasks;
    }

    @PostMapping
    public Task addTask(@RequestBody Task task) {
        tasks.add(task);
        return task;
    }
}

class Task {
    private String id;
    private String description;

    // Getters and setters
    public String getId() {
        return id;
    }

    public void setId(String id) {
        this.id = id;
    }

    public String getDescription() {
```

```java
    return description;
    }

    public void setDescription(String description) {
        this.description = description;
    }
}
```

1. **Run the Spring Boot Application**:
   - Start your application and ensure the endpoints work as expected.
   - Test the API using Postman or curl:
     - GET /api/tasks → Returns the list of tasks.
     - POST /api/tasks → Adds a new task.

Step 2: Setting Up the Frontend (React)

Install Axios for API Requests

Use Axios, a popular HTTP client for JavaScript, to handle API calls.

Install Axios:
bash
CopyEdit
```bash
npm install axios
```

1. **Create a Service for API Requests**:

Create a file named apiService.js:
javascript
CopyEdit
```javascript
import axios from "axios";

const API_BASE_URL = "http://localhost:8080/api/tasks";

const apiService = {
  getTasks: async () => {
```

```javascript
    const response = await axios.get(API_BASE_URL);
    return response.data;
  },
  addTask: async (task) => {
    const response = await axios.post(API_BASE_URL, task);
    return response.data;
  },
};

export default apiService;
```

Step 3: Connecting React to the Backend

Fetching Data from the Backend

1. **Update the React Component**:

Create a TaskList component:

javascript

CopyEdit

```javascript
import React, { useEffect, useState } from "react";
import apiService from "./apiService";

const TaskList = () => {
  const [tasks, setTasks] = useState([]);

  useEffect(() => {
    const fetchTasks = async () => {
      const data = await apiService.getTasks();
      setTasks(data);
    };

    fetchTasks();
  }, []);
```

115

```javascript
  return (
    <div>
      <h1>Task List</h1>
      <ul>
        {tasks.map((task) => (
          <li key={task.id}>{task.description}</li>
        ))}
      </ul>
    </div>
  );
};

export default TaskList;
```

2. **Test the Component**:
   o Ensure the TaskList component fetches and displays data from the backend.

Sending Data to the Backend

1. **Add a Form for Adding Tasks**:

Create a TaskForm component:
javascript
CopyEdit
```javascript
import React, { useState } from "react";
import apiService from "./apiService";

const TaskForm = ({ onTaskAdded }) => {
  const [description, setDescription] = useState("");

  const handleSubmit = async (e) => {
    e.preventDefault();
    const newTask = { id: Date.now().toString(), description };
```

```javascript
    const addedTask = await apiService.addTask(newTask);
    onTaskAdded(addedTask);
    setDescription("");
  };

  return (
    <form onSubmit={handleSubmit}>
      <input
        type="text"
        value={description}
        onChange={(e) => setDescription(e.target.value)}
        placeholder="Enter a task"
      />
      <button type="submit">Add Task</button>
    </form>
  );
};

export default TaskForm;
```

2. Combine the Components:

Update the TaskList component to include the form:

javascript

CopyEdit

```javascript
import React, { useEffect, useState } from "react";
import apiService from "./apiService";
import TaskForm from "./TaskForm";

const TaskList = () => {
  const [tasks, setTasks] = useState([]);

  useEffect(() => {
    const fetchTasks = async () => {
      const data = await apiService.getTasks();
```

```
      setTasks(data);
    };

    fetchTasks();
  }, []);

  const handleTaskAdded = (newTask) => {
    setTasks((prevTasks) => [...prevTasks, newTask]);
  };

  return (
    <div>
      <h1>Task List</h1>
      <TaskForm onTaskAdded={handleTaskAdded} />
      <ul>
        {tasks.map((task) => (
          <li key={task.id}>{task.description}</li>
        ))}
      </ul>
    </div>
  );
};

export default TaskList;
```

3. **Test Adding Tasks**:
   - Add tasks via the form and verify that they are displayed in the list.

Step 4: Handling CORS Issues

Cross-Origin Resource Sharing (CORS) errors can occur when the frontend (React) and backend (Spring Boot) run on different domains (e.g., localhost:3000 and localhost:8080).

Fixing CORS in Spring Boot

Add a CORS Configuration Class:

java

CopyEdit

```java
import org.springframework.context.annotation.Bean;
import org.springframework.context.annotation.Configuration;
import org.springframework.web.servlet.config.annotation.CorsRegistry;
import org.springframework.web.servlet.config.annotation.WebMvcConfigurer;

@Configuration
public class CorsConfig {

    @Bean
    public WebMvcConfigurer corsConfigurer() {
        return new WebMvcConfigurer() {
            @Override
            public void addCorsMappings(CorsRegistry registry) {
                registry.addMapping("/api/**")
                    .allowedOrigins("http://localhost:3000")
                        .allowedMethods("GET", "POST", "PUT", "DELETE");
            }
        };
    }
}
```

1. **Restart the Backend**:
   o Verify that CORS errors are resolved.

Step 5: Deployment Considerations

1. **Build the React App**:

Create a production build of your React app:

bash

npm run build

2. **Serve the React App via Spring Boot**:
    - Copy the contents of the build folder into the src/main/resources/static directory of your Spring Boot project.
    - Access the React app at the root URL (http://localhost:8080).

This chapter demonstrated how to connect a React frontend to a Spring Boot backend, including setting up API communication, handling CORS issues, and deploying a production-ready app. With this knowledge, you can now build powerful full-stack applications that seamlessly integrate the frontend and backend.

In the next chapter, we'll explore **Testing and Debugging Full-Stack Applications**, focusing on ensuring your application runs reliably and efficiently.

Solving CORS Issues

Cross-Origin Resource Sharing (CORS) is a security feature implemented by browsers to prevent web pages from making requests to a domain other than their own. In a typical full-stack application, the frontend (React) and backend (Spring Boot) often run on different domains or ports (e.g., localhost:3000 and localhost:8080), leading to CORS errors.

What Causes CORS Issues?

When a React app running on http://localhost:3000 tries to make an API request to a Spring Boot backend at http://localhost:8080, the browser blocks the request unless the backend explicitly allows it. This is because the browser enforces a same-origin policy, which restricts cross-origin requests.

Fixing CORS in Spring Boot

There are multiple ways to handle CORS in Spring Boot:

---

1. Global CORS Configuration

You can configure CORS for all endpoints globally.

Create a CORS Configuration Class:

java

CopyEdit

```java
import org.springframework.context.annotation.Bean;

import org.springframework.context.annotation.Configuration;

import org.springframework.web.servlet.config.annotation.CorsRegistry;

import org.springframework.web.servlet.config.annotation.WebMvcConfigurer;


@Configuration

public class CorsConfig {


    @Bean

    public WebMvcConfigurer corsConfigurer() {

        return new WebMvcConfigurer() {

            @Override

            public void addCorsMappings(CorsRegistry registry) {

                registry.addMapping("/**") // Allow all paths

                        .allowedOrigins("http://localhost:3000") // Allow React app
```

```
                    .allowedMethods("GET", "POST", "PUT", "DELETE") // Allow specific
HTTP methods

                    .allowedHeaders("*") // Allow all headers

                    .allowCredentials(true); // Allow cookies if needed

            }

        };

    }

}
```

1. **Restart the Backend**:
   - This configuration applies to all API endpoints and resolves CORS issues for most use cases.

---

2. CORS Configuration for Specific Controllers

If you want to restrict CORS to specific controllers or endpoints, use the @CrossOrigin annotation.

Example:

java

CopyEdit

```
import org.springframework.web.bind.annotation.*;


@RestController

@RequestMapping("/api/tasks")

@CrossOrigin(origins = "http://localhost:3000") // Allow requests from React app

public class TaskController {
```

```
// Controller code here

}
```

1. **Customize Options**:
   - You can specify multiple origins, methods, headers, etc.

---

3. Using Spring Security for CORS

If your Spring Boot app uses Spring Security, CORS must also be configured in the security configuration.

Example:

java

CopyEdit

```
import org.springframework.context.annotation.Bean;

import org.springframework.context.annotation.Configuration;

import org.springframework.security.config.annotation.web.builders.HttpSecurity;

import org.springframework.security.web.SecurityFilterChain;


@Configuration

public class SecurityConfig {


    @Bean

    public SecurityFilterChain securityFilterChain(HttpSecurity http) throws Exception {
        http

            .cors().and() // Enable CORS
```

123

```
    .csrf().disable() // Disable CSRF for simplicity

    .authorizeHttpRequests()

        .anyRequest().authenticated()

    .and()

    .httpBasic();

   return http.build();

  }

}
```

1. **Define a CORS Configuration Source**:
   java
   CopyEdit
   ```
   import org.springframework.context.annotation.Bean;
   ```

```
import org.springframework.web.cors.CorsConfiguration;

import org.springframework.web.cors.UrlBasedCorsConfigurationSource;

import org.springframework.web.filter.CorsFilter;


@Bean

public CorsFilter corsFilter() {

    CorsConfiguration config = new CorsConfiguration();

    config.addAllowedOrigin("http://localhost:3000");

    config.addAllowedMethod("*");

    config.addAllowedHeader("*");
```

```
UrlBasedCorsConfigurationSource source = new UrlBasedCorsConfigurationSource();

source.registerCorsConfiguration("/**", config);


return new CorsFilter(source);

}
```

Testing CORS Configuration

1. Open your React app and make an API request (e.g., using Axios).
2. If the configuration is correct, you'll no longer see CORS-related errors in the browser console.

Authentication and Securing API Calls

Once CORS is resolved, the next step is securing your API. Authentication ensures that only authorized users can access your backend, and securing API calls protects sensitive data.

Adding Authentication to API Calls

1. JWT Authentication

JSON Web Tokens (JWTs) are commonly used for securing APIs in stateless applications.

Backend: Generate JWTs: Use Spring Boot to generate JWTs during login and validate them for subsequent API requests. Example:

java

CopyEdit

```
@RestController

@RequestMapping("/auth")
```

```java
public class AuthController {


    @PostMapping("/login")

    public ResponseEntity<String> login(@RequestBody AuthRequest request) {

        // Validate user credentials (e.g., against a database)

        if (request.getUsername().equals("user") && request.getPassword().equals("password"))
{

            String token = JwtUtil.generateToken(request.getUsername());

            return ResponseEntity.ok(token);

        }

        return ResponseEntity.status(HttpStatus.UNAUTHORIZED).build();

    }

}
```

1. **Frontend: Include JWT in API Calls**:
   - Store the token in local storage or a secure cookie after login.

Include the token in the Authorization header for subsequent requests:

javascript

CopyEdit

```javascript
const fetchTasks = async () => {

    const token = localStorage.getItem("token");

    const response = await axios.get("http://localhost:8080/api/tasks", {

        headers: {

            Authorization: `Bearer ${token}`,
```

```
      },
    });

    setTasks(response.data);

};
```

Backend: Validate JWTs: Use a filter to validate JWTs for protected endpoints:
java
CopyEdit

```
@Override
protected void doFilterInternal(HttpServletRequest request, HttpServletResponse response,
FilterChain chain)
    throws ServletException, IOException {
    String header = request.getHeader("Authorization");

    if (header != null && header.startsWith("Bearer ")) {
        String token = header.substring(7);
        if (JwtUtil.validateToken(token)) {
            String username = JwtUtil.extractUsername(token);
            // Set authentication in the security context
        }
    }

    chain.doFilter(request, response);
}
```

2. OAuth2 for Social Logins

For a seamless user experience, you can enable social logins with OAuth2.

Backend: Configure OAuth2: Add the following dependency:
xml
CopyEdit

```xml
<dependency>

  <groupId>org.springframework.boot</groupId>

  <artifactId>spring-boot-starter-oauth2-client</artifactId>

</dependency>
```

1. **Set Up Social Login**: Add OAuth2 properties in application.properties:
   properties
   CopyEdit

   ```properties
   spring.security.oauth2.client.registration.google.client-id=your-client-id

   spring.security.oauth2.client.registration.google.client-secret=your-client-secret
   ```

2. **Frontend: Redirect Users**: Use React to redirect users to the social login page and handle the callback to retrieve the access token.

Best Practices for Securing API Calls

1. **Always Use HTTPS**:
   - Secure API communication with SSL/TLS to prevent data interception.
2. **Limit API Exposure**:
   - Restrict public access to sensitive endpoints.
   - Use role-based access control (RBAC).
3. **Validate User Input**:
   - Use validation frameworks to prevent injection attacks.
4. **Log and Monitor API Access**:
   - Track API usage to detect suspicious activity.

In this section, we addressed CORS issues to enable seamless frontend-backend communication and implemented authentication using JWTs and OAuth2 for securing API calls. These practices ensure that your application is both functional and secure.

In the next chapter, we'll explore **Testing and Debugging Full-Stack Applications**, focusing on how to ensure your application runs smoothly across all layers.

Chapter 9: Real-Time Features and Advanced Integration

Modern applications often require real-time features to provide instant updates and a dynamic user experience. Advanced integration techniques can further enhance the interactivity and functionality of your full-stack application. In this chapter, we'll explore implementing real-time communication using WebSockets, Server-Sent Events (SSE), and third-party APIs for advanced integration.

Real-Time Features

Real-time communication allows the server to push updates to the client without the client needing to request data repeatedly. This is crucial for features like live chat, notifications, collaborative editing, or real-time dashboards.

---

1. Using WebSockets

WebSockets provide full-duplex communication channels between the client and server, enabling instant bidirectional data transfer.

Setting Up WebSockets in Spring Boot

Add WebSocket Dependency: Add the following dependency to your pom.xml:

xml

CopyEdit

```
<dependency>
    <groupId>org.springframework.boot</groupId>
    <artifactId>spring-boot-starter-websocket</artifactId>
</dependency>
```

1. **Configure WebSocket in Spring Boot**: Create a WebSocket configuration class:
java
CopyEdit

```java
import org.springframework.context.annotation.Configuration;

import org.springframework.web.socket.config.annotation.EnableWebSocketMessageBroker;
import org.springframework.web.socket.config.annotation.StompEndpointRegistry;
import
org.springframework.web.socket.config.annotation.WebSocketMessageBrokerConfigurer;

@Configuration
@EnableWebSocketMessageBroker
public class WebSocketConfig implements WebSocketMessageBrokerConfigurer {

    @Override
    public void registerStompEndpoints(StompEndpointRegistry registry) {
        registry.addEndpoint("/ws").setAllowedOrigins("http://localhost:3000").withSockJS();
    }

    @Override
    public void
configureMessageBroker(org.springframework.messaging.simp.config.MessageBrokerRegistry registry) {
        registry.enableSimpleBroker("/topic");
        registry.setApplicationDestinationPrefixes("/app");
    }
}
```

2. **Create a WebSocket Controller**: Handle incoming messages and broadcast updates:
java
CopyEdit

```java
import org.springframework.messaging.handler.annotation.MessageMapping;
import org.springframework.messaging.handler.annotation.SendTo;
import org.springframework.stereotype.Controller;
```

131

```java
@Controller
public class ChatController {

  @MessageMapping("/chat")
  @SendTo("/topic/messages")
  public String sendMessage(String message) {
    return message;
  }
}
```

3. **Frontend: Integrate WebSockets with React**: Install a library like @stomp/stompjs for WebSocket communication:
   bash
   CopyEdit
   npm install @stomp/stompjs

Implement a simple WebSocket client in React:
javascript
CopyEdit

```javascript
import React, { useEffect, useState } from "react";
import { Client } from "@stomp/stompjs";

const ChatApp = () => {
  const [messages, setMessages] = useState([]);
  const [message, setMessage] = useState("");

  useEffect(() => {
    const client = new Client({
      brokerURL: "ws://localhost:8080/ws",
      onConnect: () => {
        client.subscribe("/topic/messages", (message) => {
          setMessages((prev) => [...prev, message.body]);
        });
```

```
      },
    });

    client.activate();

    return () => client.deactivate();
  }, []);

  const sendMessage = () => {
    const client = new Client({
      brokerURL: "ws://localhost:8080/ws",
    });
    client.activate();
    client.publish({ destination: "/app/chat", body: message });
    setMessage("");
  };

  return (
    <div>
      <ul>
        {messages.map((msg, index) => (
          <li key={index}>{msg}</li>
        ))}
      </ul>
      <input
        value={message}
        onChange={(e) => setMessage(e.target.value)}
        placeholder="Type a message"
      />
      <button onClick={sendMessage}>Send</button>
    </div>
  );
};
```

export default ChatApp;

---

2. Using Server-Sent Events (SSE)

SSE is a simpler alternative to WebSockets for server-to-client one-way communication.

Setting Up SSE in Spring Boot

Create an SSE Controller:

java

CopyEdit

```
import org.springframework.web.bind.annotation.GetMapping;
import org.springframework.web.bind.annotation.RestController;
import org.springframework.web.servlet.mvc.method.annotation.SseEmitter;

import java.io.IOException;

@RestController
public class SseController {

    @GetMapping("/stream")
    public SseEmitter stream() {
        SseEmitter emitter = new SseEmitter();
        new Thread(() -> {
            try {
                for (int i = 0; i < 10; i++) {
                    emitter.send("Event " + i);
                    Thread.sleep(1000);
                }
                emitter.complete();
            } catch (IOException | InterruptedException e) {
                emitter.completeWithError(e);
            }
        }).start();
        return emitter;
```

```
}
}
```

1. **Frontend: Consume SSE in React**: Use the browser's EventSource API:
   javascript
   CopyEdit
   ```javascript
   import React, { useEffect, useState } from "react";

   const SseComponent = () => {
     const [events, setEvents] = useState([]);

     useEffect(() => {
       const eventSource = new EventSource("http://localhost:8080/stream");
       eventSource.onmessage = (event) => {
         setEvents((prev) => [...prev, event.data]);
       };

       return () => eventSource.close();
     }, []);

     return (
       <div>
         <ul>
           {events.map((event, index) => (
             <li key={index}>{event}</li>
           ))}
         </ul>
       </div>
     );
   };

   export default SseComponent;
   ```

2. **Advanced Integration**

1. Integrating Third-Party APIs

Modern applications often rely on external APIs for additional functionality, such as payment processing, weather data, or geolocation.

1. **Example: Fetching Weather Data**:
   - Use the OpenWeather API to fetch weather information.

Backend (Spring Boot):

java

CopyEdit

```java
import org.springframework.web.bind.annotation.GetMapping;
import org.springframework.web.bind.annotation.RestController;
import org.springframework.web.client.RestTemplate;

@RestController
public class WeatherController {

    @GetMapping("/api/weather")
    public String getWeather() {
        String apiKey = "your_api_key";
        String url = "https://api.openweathermap.org/data/2.5/weather?q=London&appid=" + apiKey;
        RestTemplate restTemplate = new RestTemplate();
        return restTemplate.getForObject(url, String.class);
    }
}
```

Frontend (React):

javascript

CopyEdit

```javascript
import React, { useEffect, useState } from "react";
import axios from "axios";
```

```
const Weather = () => {
  const [weather, setWeather] = useState("");

  useEffect(() => {
    const fetchWeather = async () => {
      const response = await axios.get("http://localhost:8080/api/weather");
      setWeather(response.data);
    };

    fetchWeather();
  }, []);

  return <div>{weather}</div>;
};

export default Weather;
```

---

2. Implementing Payment Gateways

Payment integration is essential for e-commerce applications.

1. **Stripe Integration:**

Backend:
java
CopyEdit

```
import com.stripe.Stripe;
import com.stripe.model.checkout.Session;
import com.stripe.param.checkout.SessionCreateParams;
import org.springframework.web.bind.annotation.PostMapping;
import org.springframework.web.bind.annotation.RestController;

@RestController
public class PaymentController {
```

137

```java
@PostMapping("/api/checkout")
public String checkout() throws Exception {
    Stripe.apiKey = "your_secret_key";

    SessionCreateParams params = SessionCreateParams.builder()
        .setMode(SessionCreateParams.Mode.PAYMENT)
        .setSuccessUrl("http://localhost:3000/success")
        .setCancelUrl("http://localhost:3000/cancel")
        .addLineItem(
            SessionCreateParams.LineItem.builder()
                .setQuantity(1L)
                .setPriceData(
                    SessionCreateParams.LineItem.PriceData.builder()
                        .setCurrency("usd")
                        .setUnitAmount(2000L)
                        .setProductData(
                            SessionCreateParams.LineItem.PriceData.ProductData.builder()
                                .setName("Sample Product")
                                .build())
                        .build())
                .build())
        .build();

    Session session = Session.create(params);
    return session.getUrl();
}
}
```

Frontend:

javascript

CopyEdit

```javascript
import React from "react";
import axios from "axios";
```

```
const Checkout = () => {
    const handleCheckout = async () => {
        const { data } = await axios.post("http://localhost:8080/api/checkout");
        window.location.href = data;
    };

    return <button onClick={handleCheckout}>Checkout</button>;
};

export default Checkout;
```

This section introduced real-time communication using WebSockets and SSE, along with advanced integration techniques like third-party APIs and payment gateways. These tools and strategies enable developers to create dynamic, interactive, and feature-rich full-stack applications.

In the next chapter, we'll explore **Testing and Debugging Full-Stack Applications**, focusing on ensuring your application performs reliably and efficiently.

Building Real-Time Applications with WebSockets

Real-time applications require instant communication between clients and servers. WebSockets enable bidirectional communication, allowing servers to send updates to clients as events happen. This is particularly useful for live chat, notifications, collaborative tools, or dashboards.

How WebSockets Work

WebSockets establish a persistent connection between the client and server over a single TCP connection. Unlike HTTP, WebSockets avoid the overhead of establishing a new connection for every request, making them faster and more efficient for real-time communication.

Setting Up WebSocket Communication in Spring Boot

Add WebSocket Dependency: Include the WebSocket starter in your pom.xml:

xml

CopyEdit

```
<dependency>

    <groupId>org.springframework.boot</groupId>

    <artifactId>spring-boot-starter-websocket</artifactId>

</dependency>
```

1. **Enable WebSocket Message Broker**: Configure WebSocket support in Spring Boot:

   java

   CopyEdit

   ```
   import org.springframework.context.annotation.Configuration;

   import org.springframework.web.socket.config.annotation.EnableWebSocketMessageBroker;

   import org.springframework.web.socket.config.annotation.StompEndpointRegistry;

   import org.springframework.web.socket.config.annotation.WebSocketMessageBrokerConfigurer;


   @Configuration

   @EnableWebSocketMessageBroker

   public class WebSocketConfig implements WebSocketMessageBrokerConfigurer {
   ```

```java
@Override

public void registerStompEndpoints(StompEndpointRegistry registry) {

    registry.addEndpoint("/ws").setAllowedOrigins("http://localhost:3000").withSockJS();

}


@Override

public void
configureMessageBroker(org.springframework.messaging.simp.config.MessageBrokerRegistry registry) {

    registry.enableSimpleBroker("/topic");

    registry.setApplicationDestinationPrefixes("/app");

}

}
```

2.
  - /ws: The endpoint for WebSocket connections.
  - /topic: Destination for messages broadcast to clients.
  - /app: Prefix for client-to-server communication.

Create a WebSocket Controller: Handle messages sent by clients and broadcast updates:
java
CopyEdit

```java
import org.springframework.messaging.handler.annotation.MessageMapping;

import org.springframework.messaging.handler.annotation.SendTo;

import org.springframework.stereotype.Controller;
```

```java
@Controller

public class WebSocketController {


    @MessageMapping("/message")

    @SendTo("/topic/messages")

    public String processMessage(String message) {

        return message; // Broadcast the message to all subscribers

    }

}
```

3. **Start the Spring Boot Server**: Run your Spring Boot application to enable WebSocket communication.

Implementing WebSocket Communication in React

Install a WebSocket Library: Install @stomp/stompjs for WebSocket communication:
bash
CopyEdit
npm install @stomp/stompjs

1. **Create a WebSocket Client**: Implement WebSocket functionality in a React component:
   javascript
   CopyEdit
   import React, { useEffect, useState } from "react";

import { Client } from "@stomp/stompjs";

```javascript
const WebSocketChat = () => {

  const [messages, setMessages] = useState([]);

  const [message, setMessage] = useState("");


  useEffect(() => {

    const client = new Client({

      brokerURL: "ws://localhost:8080/ws",

      onConnect: () => {

        client.subscribe("/topic/messages", (msg) => {

          setMessages((prev) => [...prev, msg.body]);

        });

      },

    });


    client.activate();


    return () => client.deactivate();

  }, []);


  const sendMessage = () => {
```

```
const client = new Client({

  brokerURL: "ws://localhost:8080/ws",

});

client.activate();

client.publish({ destination: "/app/message", body: message });

setMessage("");

};


return (

  <div>

    <h1>WebSocket Chat</h1>

    <div>

      <ul>

        {messages.map((msg, index) => (

          <li key={index}>{msg}</li>

        ))}

      </ul>

    </div>

    <input

      type="text"

      value={message}
```

```
        onChange={(e) => setMessage(e.target.value)}

        placeholder="Type a message"

      />

      <button onClick={sendMessage}>Send</button>

    </div>

  );

};


export default WebSocketChat;
```

2. **Test the Application**:
   o Open the React app and send messages.
   o Open multiple browser tabs to simulate multiple clients and see real-time communication.

Implementing Live Chat and Notifications

Live chat and notifications are among the most common real-time features in modern applications. They can be implemented using WebSockets to push updates instantly to users.

Building a Live Chat Application

Backend: Extend WebSocket Controller: Add functionality to broadcast messages to specific users or groups:

java

CopyEdit

```
import org.springframework.messaging.handler.annotation.MessageMapping;
```

```java
import org.springframework.messaging.handler.annotation.SendTo;

import org.springframework.stereotype.Controller;


@Controller

public class ChatController {


    @MessageMapping("/chat")

    @SendTo("/topic/chat")

    public ChatMessage sendMessage(ChatMessage message) {

        return message; // Broadcast message to all subscribers

    }

}


class ChatMessage {

    private String sender;

    private String content;


    // Getters and Setters

    public String getSender() {

        return sender;

    }
```

```java
public void setSender(String sender) {

    this.sender = sender;

}


public String getContent() {

    return content;

}


public void setContent(String content) {

    this.content = content;

    }

}
```

1. **Frontend: Create a Chat Interface**: Build a chat component in React:
   javascript
   CopyEdit

```javascript
import React, { useEffect, useState } from "react";

import { Client } from "@stomp/stompjs";


const LiveChat = () => {

  const [messages, setMessages] = useState([]);

  const [message, setMessage] = useState("");

  const [username, setUsername] = useState("");
```

```
useEffect(() => {

  const client = new Client({

    brokerURL: "ws://localhost:8080/ws",

    onConnect: () => {

      client.subscribe("/topic/chat", (msg) => {

        setMessages((prev) => [...prev, JSON.parse(msg.body)]);

      });

    },

  });


  client.activate();


  return () => client.deactivate();
}, []);


const sendMessage = () => {

  const client = new Client({

    brokerURL: "ws://localhost:8080/ws",

  });

  client.activate();
```

```
client.publish({

  destination: "/app/chat",

  body: JSON.stringify({ sender: username, content: message }),

});

setMessage("");

};


return (

<div>

  <h1>Live Chat</h1>

  <div>

    <ul>

      {messages.map((msg, index) => (

        <li key={index}>

          <strong>{msg.sender}:</strong> {msg.content}

        </li>

      ))}

    </ul>

  </div>

  <input

    type="text"
```

```
      placeholder="Your Name"

      value={username}

      onChange={(e) => setUsername(e.target.value)}

    />

    <input

      type="text"

      placeholder="Type a message"

      value={message}

      onChange={(e) => setMessage(e.target.value)}

    />

    <button onClick={sendMessage}>Send</button>

  </div>

);

};


export default LiveChat;
```

2. **Implementing Notifications**

Backend: Push Notifications: Add an endpoint to send notifications via WebSockets:
java
CopyEdit
```
import org.springframework.messaging.simp.SimpMessagingTemplate;

import org.springframework.web.bind.annotation.PostMapping;

import org.springframework.web.bind.annotation.RestController;
```

```java
@RestController

public class NotificationController {

    private final SimpMessagingTemplate messagingTemplate;

    public NotificationController(SimpMessagingTemplate messagingTemplate) {
        this.messagingTemplate = messagingTemplate;
    }

    @PostMapping("/api/notify")
    public void sendNotification(String message) {
        messagingTemplate.convertAndSend("/topic/notifications", message);
    }
}
```

1. **Frontend: Subscribe to Notifications**: Subscribe to the /topic/notifications topic in React:
   javascript
   CopyEdit

```javascript
const Notifications = () => {

const [notifications, setNotifications] = useState([]);


useEffect(() => {
```

```
const client = new Client({

  brokerURL: "ws://localhost:8080/ws",

  onConnect: () => {

    client.subscribe("/topic/notifications", (msg) => {

      setNotifications((prev) => [...prev, msg.body]);

    });

  },

});


client.activate();


return () => client.deactivate();
}, []);


return (
  <div>
    <h1>Notifications</h1>
    <ul>
      {notifications.map((notif, index) => (
        <li key={index}>{notif}</li>
      ))}
```

```
        </ul>

      </div>

    );

  };


export default Notifications;
```

This section demonstrated how to implement real-time features using WebSockets for live chat and notifications. These features enhance user interactivity and are essential for modern applications. By leveraging React and Spring Boot, you can build scalable real-time systems that provide instant updates to users.

In the next chapter, we'll explore **Testing and Debugging Full-Stack Applications**, ensuring your application functions reliably across all layers.

Chapter 10: Deploying Full-Stack Applications

Preparing React for Production Builds

Deploying a full-stack application involves making both the frontend (React) and backend (Spring Boot) ready for production. In this chapter, we'll focus on creating an optimized React production build, integrating it with Spring Boot, and deploying the full application to a server.

Step 1: Building a Production-Ready React Application

Before deployment, you need to create a production build of your React app. A production build optimizes the code for performance, minifies assets, and prepares the app for deployment.

1. Run the Build Command

Navigate to your React project directory:

bash

CopyEdit

```
cd your-react-app
```

1. Run the build command:

   bash

   CopyEdit

   ```
   npm run build
   ```

2. React will generate a build folder containing the following:
   - index.html: The entry point for your application.
   - **Static files**: Minified CSS, JavaScript, and images in the static folder.

2. Verify the Build

Test the production build locally using a simple HTTP server:

bash

npm install -g serve

serve -s build

- Open the app in your browser at http://localhost:5000.

Step 2: Serving React with Spring Boot

To deploy the full-stack application as a single unit, the React app can be served by the Spring Boot backend.

1. Copy the React Build to Spring Boot

After running npm run build, copy the contents of the build folder into the src/main/resources/static directory of your Spring Boot project.

bash

cp -r your-react-app/build/* spring-boot-app/src/main/resources/static

1. When Spring Boot is started, it will serve the React app from the static directory at the root URL (http://localhost:8080).

---

2. Configure Spring Boot to Serve React

Spring Boot automatically serves static files placed in the src/main/resources/static directory. However, for React routes (e.g., /dashboard), additional configuration is required to handle client-side routing.

Add a Controller for React Routing:

java

import org.springframework.stereotype.Controller;

import org.springframework.web.bind.annotation.RequestMapping;

@Controller

public class ReactController {

```
@RequestMapping("/{path:[^\\.]*}")
public String redirect() {
    // Forward all non-API routes to index.html
    return "forward:/index.html";
}
}
```

- This controller forwards all non-API routes (excluding routes with file extensions like .js or .css) to the React index.html.

Step 3: Preparing Spring Boot for Production

To ensure the backend is production-ready, make the following adjustments:

1. Configure a Production Database

Replace the in-memory H2 database with a production database (e.g., MySQL or PostgreSQL).

Add the Database Dependency:

xml

CopyEdit

```
<dependency>
    <groupId>org.springframework.boot</groupId>
    <artifactId>spring-boot-starter-data-jpa</artifactId>
</dependency>
<dependency>
    <groupId>mysql</groupId>
    <artifactId>mysql-connector-java</artifactId>
</dependency>
```

1. **Update** application.properties:

   properties

   CopyEdit

   spring.datasource.url=jdbc:mysql://localhost:3306/your_database

spring.datasource.username=your_username

spring.datasource.password=your_password

spring.jpa.hibernate.ddl-auto=update

2. **Verify the Database Connection**: Start your Spring Boot app and ensure it connects to the production database.

---

2. Optimize Application Properties

Create separate profiles for development and production by using application-dev.properties and application-prod.properties.

Specify Active Profile: In application.properties, set the active profile:

properties

CopyEdit

spring.profiles.active=prod

1. **Example Production Configuration**:

   properties

   CopyEdit

   server.port=8080

logging.level.root=WARN

logging.file.name=logs/app.log

---

3. Build the Spring Boot Jar

Package the Spring Boot application as an executable jar:

bash

CopyEdit

```
mvn clean package
```

The jar file will be generated in the target folder.

Step 4: Deploying to a Server

Once the React and Spring Boot applications are production-ready, deploy them to a cloud server or hosting provider.

1. Deploying on AWS EC2

1. **Launch an EC2 Instance**:
   - Choose an Amazon Linux or Ubuntu AMI.
   - Configure security groups to allow traffic on ports 8080 (backend) and 80/443 (frontend).
2. **Install Java**:

Update the package manager:
bash
CopyEdit
```
sudo apt update
```
Install OpenJDK:
bash
CopyEdit
```
sudo apt install openjdk-11-jdk
```
3. **Copy the Jar File to the Server**:

Use scp to copy the jar file:
bash
CopyEdit
```
scp target/app.jar ec2-user@your-ec2-ip:/home/ec2-user
```

Run the Spring Boot Application:

bash

CopyEdit

java -jar app.jar

4.

5. **Access the Application**:

   o The backend and React app will be accessible at the server's public IP (e.g., http://your-ec2-ip:8080).

---

2. Deploying on Docker

Docker simplifies deployment by containerizing the application.

Create a Dockerfile:

dockerfile

CopyEdit

```
# Stage 1: Build React app
FROM node:14 as build
WORKDIR /app
COPY your-react-app .
RUN npm install
RUN npm run build

# Stage 2: Build Spring Boot app
FROM openjdk:11
WORKDIR /app
COPY spring-boot-app/target/app.jar .
COPY --from=build /app/build /static
CMD ["java", "-jar", "app.jar"]
```

Build and Run the Docker Image:

bash

CopyEdit

```
docker build -t fullstack-app .
docker run -p 8080:8080 fullstack-app
```

1. **Access the Application**:
   - **Open** http://localhost:8080.

Step 5: Configuring Nginx for Reverse Proxy

If you want to serve the frontend and backend under a single domain, configure Nginx as a reverse proxy.

Install Nginx:

bash

CopyEdit

```
sudo apt install nginx
```

1. **Configure Nginx**: Create a configuration file (e.g., /etc/nginx/sites-available/fullstack-app):

   nginx

   CopyEdit

   ```
   server {
   ```

```
listen 80;
server_name your-domain.com;

location / {
    root /var/www/html;
    index index.html;
    try_files $uri /index.html;
}

location /api/ {
```

```
    proxy_pass http://localhost:8080/;
    proxy_set_header Host $host;
    proxy_set_header X-Real-IP $remote_addr;
    proxy_set_header X-Forwarded-For $proxy_add_x_forwarded_for;
  }
}
```

Enable the Configuration:

bash

CopyEdit

```
sudo ln -s /etc/nginx/sites-available/fullstack-app /etc/nginx/sites-enabled/
sudo systemctl restart nginx
```

This chapter outlined the process of preparing your React app for production, serving it with Spring Boot, and deploying the full-stack application to a server. By following these steps, you can deploy a secure, efficient, and production-ready full-stack application.

Next, we'll focus on **Testing and Debugging Full-Stack Applications**, ensuring your application runs smoothly and efficiently in production.

Deploying Spring Boot Applications to AWS or GCP

Cloud platforms like AWS and Google Cloud Platform (GCP) offer robust solutions for hosting full-stack applications. In this section, we'll cover how to deploy a Spring Boot application to **AWS EC2** and **GCP Compute Engine**.

---

1. Deploying Spring Boot to AWS EC2

Step 1: Launch an EC2 Instance

1. Go to the AWS Management Console.
2. Launch an EC2 instance:
   - Choose **Amazon Linux 2** or **Ubuntu** as the operating system.
   - Select an instance type (e.g., t2.micro for free-tier eligible).
   - Configure security groups to allow traffic on port 8080 for your Spring Boot application and 22 for SSH access.

Step 2: Install Java on the Instance

SSH into the instance:

bash

CopyEdit

```
ssh -i your-key.pem ec2-user@your-ec2-ip
```

1. Install OpenJDK:

   bash

   CopyEdit

   ```
   sudo yum update -y
   ```

```
sudo yum install java-11-openjdk-devel -y
```

Confirm Java installation:

bash

CopyEdit

```
java -version
```

Step 3: Transfer Your Spring Boot Jar

Use scp to copy the Spring Boot jar file to the EC2 instance:

bash

CopyEdit

```
scp -i your-key.pem target/app.jar ec2-user@your-ec2-ip:/home/ec2-user
```

Step 4: Run the Spring Boot Application

Start the application:

bash

CopyEdit

```
java -jar app.jar
```

1. Access the application via http://your-ec2-ip:8080.

Step 5: Configure the Application as a Service

Create a systemd service to manage the Spring Boot application:

bash

CopyEdit

```
sudo nano /etc/systemd/system/springboot.service
```

Add the following content:

ini

CopyEdit

```
[Unit]

Description=Spring Boot Application

After=network.target


[Service]
```

163

User=ec2-user

ExecStart=/usr/bin/java -jar /home/ec2-user/app.jar

Restart=always

[Install]

WantedBy=multi-user.target

1. Reload systemd and start the service:
   bash
   CopyEdit
   sudo systemctl daemon-reload

sudo systemctl start springboot

sudo systemctl enable springboot

---

2. Deploying Spring Boot to GCP Compute Engine

Step 1: Create a VM Instance

1. Go to the Google Cloud Console.
2. Create a new Compute Engine instance:
   - Choose a machine type (e.g., e2-micro for free-tier eligible).
   - Select an image like **Debian** or **Ubuntu**.
   - Configure the firewall to allow traffic on port 8080.

Step 2: Install Java

SSH into the instance from the GCP Console or using gcloud:
bash

CopyEdit

```
gcloud compute ssh instance-name --zone=zone-name
```

1. Install OpenJDK:

   bash

   CopyEdit

   ```
   sudo apt update
   ```

```
sudo apt install openjdk-11-jdk -y
```

Confirm Java installation:

bash

CopyEdit

```
java -version
```

Step 3: Transfer and Run the Application

Upload the jar file using gcloud:

bash

CopyEdit

```
gcloud compute scp target/app.jar instance-name:/home/username --zone=zone-name
```

1. Start the application:

   bash

   CopyEdit

   ```
   java -jar app.jar
   ```

2. Access the application at http://instance-external-ip:8080.

Step 4: Set Up Auto-Start To ensure the application restarts automatically after a reboot, use systemd as described in the AWS EC2 section.

Dockerizing Full-Stack Applications

Docker provides a simple way to package and deploy applications in isolated environments. By containerizing both the React frontend and Spring Boot backend, you can deploy your full-stack application consistently across different platforms.

Step 1: Create a Dockerfile for Spring Boot

Dockerfile: Create a Dockerfile in the root of your Spring Boot project:

dockerfile

CopyEdit

```
# Use an OpenJDK base image

FROM openjdk:11-jre

WORKDIR /app

# Copy the jar file

COPY target/app.jar app.jar

# Expose port 8080

EXPOSE 8080

# Command to run the application

ENTRYPOINT ["java", "-jar", "app.jar"]
```

1. **Build the Docker Image**:
   bash
   CopyEdit
   ```
   docker build -t springboot-app .
   ```

2. **Run the Container**:

bash

CopyEdit

```
docker run -p 8080:8080 springboot-app
```

Step 2: Create a Dockerfile for React

Dockerfile: Create a Dockerfile in the root of your React project:

dockerfile

CopyEdit

```
# Use a Node.js image to build the app

FROM node:14 as build

WORKDIR /app

COPY package*.json ./

RUN npm install

COPY . .

RUN npm run build


# Use a lightweight server to serve the app

FROM nginx:alpine

COPY --from=build /app/build /usr/share/nginx/html

EXPOSE 80

CMD ["nginx", "-g", "daemon off;"]
```

1. **Build the Docker Image**:
   bash
   CopyEdit
   docker build -t react-app .

2. **Run the Container**:
   bash
   CopyEdit
   docker run -p 80:80 react-app

Step 3: Create a Docker Compose File

Docker Compose allows you to manage multi-container applications with a single configuration file.

docker-compose.yml: Create a docker-compose.yml file in the root of your project:
yaml
CopyEdit
version: "3.8"

services:

  backend:

    build:

      context: ./springboot-app

    ports:

      - "8080:8080"

  frontend:

    build:

      context: ./react-app

ports:

- "3000:80"

depends_on:

- backend

1. **Start the Application**: Run both containers with a single command:
   bash
   CopyEdit
   docker-compose up --build

2. **Access the Application**:
   - Frontend: http://localhost:3000
   - Backend: http://localhost:8080

Step 4: Deploy Containers to AWS or GCP

Deploy to AWS ECS

1. **Push Docker Images to Amazon ECR**:
   - Create an ECR repository.

Tag and push your images:
bash
CopyEdit
docker tag springboot-app:latest your-ecr-url/springboot-app:latest

docker tag react-app:latest your-ecr-url/react-app:latest

docker push your-ecr-url/springboot-app:latest

docker push your-ecr-url/react-app:latest

2. **Create an ECS Cluster**:
   - ○ Use the AWS ECS Console or CLI to set up a cluster.
   - ○ Deploy your containers using the images pushed to ECR.

Deploy to GCP Cloud Run

Push Docker Images to Google Container Registry:
bash
CopyEdit
docker tag springboot-app gcr.io/your-project-id/springboot-app

docker tag react-app gcr.io/your-project-id/react-app

docker push gcr.io/your-project-id/springboot-app

docker push gcr.io/your-project-id/react-app

1. **Deploy to Cloud Run**:

Use the GCP Console or CLI:
bash
CopyEdit
gcloud run deploy springboot-app --image gcr.io/your-project-id/springboot-app --platform managed --region us-central1

gcloud run deploy react-app --image gcr.io/your-project-id/react-app --platform managed --region us-central1

This section covered deploying Spring Boot applications to AWS EC2 and GCP Compute Engine and dockerizing full-stack applications for consistent deployment. You also learned how to use Docker Compose for multi-container applications and deploy containers to cloud platforms like AWS ECS and GCP Cloud Run. By containerizing your applications, you ensure portability, scalability, and ease of deployment.

In the next chapter, we'll focus on **Testing and Debugging Full-Stack Applications** to ensure your deployed applications run reliably in production.

Chapter 11: Testing and Debugging

Unit Testing Spring Boot with JUnit and Mockito

Testing is an essential aspect of software development that ensures your application works as intended. In this chapter, we'll focus on writing unit tests for your Spring Boot application using **JUnit** and **Mockito**, two widely-used testing frameworks.

Why Unit Testing?

Unit testing involves testing individual components (e.g., classes, methods) in isolation to ensure they perform as expected. Benefits include:

1. Catching bugs early in development.
2. Facilitating refactoring without fear of breaking functionality.
3. Providing documentation on how components should behave.

Setting Up JUnit and Mockito

Add Dependencies to pom.xml: Include JUnit 5 (default in Spring Boot) and Mockito:

xml

CopyEdit

```
<dependency>
  <groupId>org.springframework.boot</groupId>
  <artifactId>spring-boot-starter-test</artifactId>
  <scope>test</scope>
  <exclusions>
    <exclusion>
      <groupId>org.junit.vintage</groupId>
      <artifactId>junit-vintage-engine</artifactId>
    </exclusion>
  </exclusions>
```

```
</dependency>
<dependency>
  <groupId>org.mockito</groupId>
  <artifactId>mockito-core</artifactId>
  <scope>test</scope>
</dependency>
```

- spring-boot-starter-test: Includes JUnit 5, Mockito, and other testing utilities.
- **Exclude** junit-vintage-engine to avoid running JUnit 4 tests if not required.

Structure of Unit Tests

- Test files are placed in the src/test/java directory.
- Each test class should correspond to a class in your main codebase.
- Common naming conventions:
  - Production class: TaskService.java
  - Test class: TaskServiceTest.java

Writing Unit Tests with JUnit

Testing a Service Class: Let's test a TaskService class that contains business logic for managing tasks.

TaskService.java:

java

CopyEdit

```java
package com.example.demo.service;

import com.example.demo.model.Task;
import com.example.demo.repository.TaskRepository;
import org.springframework.stereotype.Service;

import java.util.List;
```

```java
@Service
public class TaskService {
    private final TaskRepository taskRepository;

    public TaskService(TaskRepository taskRepository) {
        this.taskRepository = taskRepository;
    }

    public List<Task> getAllTasks() {
        return taskRepository.findAll();
    }

    public Task addTask(Task task) {
        return taskRepository.save(task);
    }
}
```

TaskServiceTest.java:

java

CopyEdit

```java
package com.example.demo.service;

import com.example.demo.model.Task;
import com.example.demo.repository.TaskRepository;
import org.junit.jupiter.api.BeforeEach;
import org.junit.jupiter.api.Test;
import org.mockito.InjectMocks;
import org.mockito.Mock;
import org.mockito.MockitoAnnotations;

import java.util.Arrays;
import java.util.List;

import static org.junit.jupiter.api.Assertions.assertEquals;
import static org.mockito.Mockito.*;
```

174

```java
class TaskServiceTest {

    @Mock
    private TaskRepository taskRepository;

    @InjectMocks
    private TaskService taskService;

    @BeforeEach
    void setUp() {
        MockitoAnnotations.openMocks(this); // Initialize mocks
    }

    @Test
    void testGetAllTasks() {
        // Arrange
        List<Task> mockTasks = Arrays.asList(
            new Task(1L, "Task 1"),
            new Task(2L, "Task 2")
        );
        when(taskRepository.findAll()).thenReturn(mockTasks);

        // Act
        List<Task> tasks = taskService.getAllTasks();

        // Assert
        assertEquals(2, tasks.size());
        verify(taskRepository, times(1)).findAll();
    }

    @Test
    void testAddTask() {
        // Arrange
```

```java
Task newTask = new Task(3L, "Task 3");
when(taskRepository.save(newTask)).thenReturn(newTask);

// Act
Task savedTask = taskService.addTask(newTask);

// Assert
assertEquals("Task 3", savedTask.getDescription());
verify(taskRepository, times(1)).save(newTask);
    }
}
```

1. **Explanation**:
   - @Mock: Creates a mock instance of the TaskRepository.
   - @InjectMocks: Injects the mocked TaskRepository into the TaskService.
   - MockitoAnnotations.openMocks(this): Initializes the mocks.
   - when(...).thenReturn(...): Defines behavior for the mock.
   - verify(...): Ensures a specific method was called.

Mocking Dependencies with Mockito

Mockito is ideal for mocking dependencies in isolation. For example:

- Mocking a database repository to avoid interacting with a real database.
- Simulating external service calls.

Example: Mocking External API Calls: Suppose your service fetches data from an external API using RestTemplate.

ExternalService.java:

java
CopyEdit
```java
package com.example.demo.service;
```

```java
import org.springframework.stereotype.Service;
import org.springframework.web.client.RestTemplate;

@Service
public class ExternalService {
    private final RestTemplate restTemplate;

    public ExternalService(RestTemplate restTemplate) {
        this.restTemplate = restTemplate;
    }

    public String fetchData(String url) {
        return restTemplate.getForObject(url, String.class);
    }
}
```

ExternalServiceTest.java:

java

CopyEdit

```java
package com.example.demo.service;

import org.junit.jupiter.api.Test;
import org.mockito.InjectMocks;
import org.mockito.Mock;
import org.mockito.MockitoAnnotations;
import org.springframework.web.client.RestTemplate;

import static org.junit.jupiter.api.Assertions.assertEquals;
import static org.mockito.Mockito.*;

class ExternalServiceTest {
```

```java
    @Mock
    private RestTemplate restTemplate;

    @InjectMocks
    private ExternalService externalService;

    @Test
    void testFetchData() {
        // Arrange
        String url = "http://example.com/api/data";
        String mockResponse = "Mock Data";
        when(restTemplate.getForObject(url, String.class)).thenReturn(mockResponse);

        // Act
        String result = externalService.fetchData(url);

        // Assert
        assertEquals("Mock Data", result);
        verify(restTemplate, times(1)).getForObject(url, String.class);
    }
}
```

Writing Tests for Controllers

Controller Class: TaskController.java:

java

CopyEdit

```java
@RestController
@RequestMapping("/api/tasks")
public class TaskController {

    private final TaskService taskService;
```

```java
public TaskController(TaskService taskService) {
    this.taskService = taskService;
}

@GetMapping
public List<Task> getAllTasks() {
    return taskService.getAllTasks();
}

@PostMapping
public Task addTask(@RequestBody Task task) {
    return taskService.addTask(task);
}
}
```

1. **Test Class**: **TaskControllerTest.java**:
   java
   CopyEdit
   ```java
   import com.example.demo.service.TaskService;
   ```

```java
import org.junit.jupiter.api.Test;
import org.mockito.InjectMocks;
import org.mockito.Mock;
import org.springframework.http.MediaType;
import org.springframework.test.web.servlet.MockMvc;
import org.springframework.test.web.servlet.setup.MockMvcBuilders;

import java.util.Arrays;

import static org.mockito.Mockito.*;
import static org.springframework.test.web.servlet.request.MockMvcRequestBuilders.*;
import static org.springframework.test.web.servlet.result.MockMvcResultMatchers.*;

class TaskControllerTest {
```

```java
@Mock
private TaskService taskService;

@InjectMocks
private TaskController taskController;

private MockMvc mockMvc;

@Test
void testGetAllTasks() throws Exception {
    mockMvc = MockMvcBuilders.standaloneSetup(taskController).build();

    when(taskService.getAllTasks()).thenReturn(
        Arrays.asList(new Task(1L, "Task 1"), new Task(2L, "Task 2"))
    );

    mockMvc.perform(get("/api/tasks"))
        .andExpect(status().isOk())
        .andExpect(jsonPath("$.length()").value(2))
        .andExpect(jsonPath("$[0].description").value("Task 1"));

    verify(taskService, times(1)).getAllTasks();
}
}
```

2. **Explanation**:
   - **MockMvc**: Simulates HTTP requests to test controller endpoints.
   - **jsonPath**: Validates JSON responses.

Best Practices for Unit Testing

1. Write tests for all critical methods and edge cases.
2. Use meaningful test names (e.g., testGetAllTasks).
3. Keep tests isolated by mocking external dependencies.
4. Run tests frequently to catch issues early.
5. Measure test coverage with tools like **JaCoCo** or **SonarQube**.

Unit testing with JUnit and Mockito ensures your Spring Boot application behaves as expected. By testing services, controllers, and external integrations in isolation, you build confidence in your code and reduce bugs. In the next section, we'll explore **Integration Testing and Debugging Full-Stack Applications**, covering how to test the entire system and diagnose complex issues.

Testing React Components with Jest and React Testing Library

Testing React components ensures your user interface behaves as expected and catches bugs in your UI logic. **Jest** is a popular JavaScript testing framework, and **React Testing Library** provides tools for testing React components in a way that mimics user interactions.

Setting Up Jest and React Testing Library

Install Dependencies: If you used Create React App, Jest is already installed. Add React Testing Library:
bash
CopyEdit
npm install @testing-library/react @testing-library/jest-dom --save-dev

1. **Add Testing Scripts**: Ensure your package.json has the following script:
   json
   CopyEdit
   "scripts": {

```
"test": "react-scripts test"

}
```

2. **Basic Folder Structure**: Place your tests in a __tests__ folder or alongside your components with a .test.js extension.

Writing Unit Tests for React Components

Example: Testing a Simple Component

Counter.js:

javascript

CopyEdit

```javascript
import React, { useState } from "react";


const Counter = () => {
  const [count, setCount] = useState(0);


  return (
    <div>
      <h1>Count: {count}</h1>
      <button onClick={() => setCount(count + 1)}>Increment</button>
      <button onClick={() => setCount(count - 1)}>Decrement</button>
    </div>
  );
```

};

export default Counter;

Counter.test.js:

javascript

CopyEdit

```
import React from "react";
import { render, screen, fireEvent } from "@testing-library/react";
import "@testing-library/jest-dom";
import Counter from "./Counter";

test("renders the counter with initial value", () => {
  render(<Counter />);
  expect(screen.getByText("Count: 0")).toBeInTheDocument();
});

test("increments the counter when the increment button is clicked", () => {
  render(<Counter />);
  const incrementButton = screen.getByText("Increment");
  fireEvent.click(incrementButton);
```

```
expect(screen.getByText("Count: 1")).toBeInTheDocument();
```

```
});
```

```
test("decrements the counter when the decrement button is clicked", () => {
```

```
render(<Counter />);
```

```
const decrementButton = screen.getByText("Decrement");
```

```
fireEvent.click(decrementButton);
```

```
expect(screen.getByText("Count: -1")).toBeInTheDocument();
```

```
});
```

Key Features of React Testing Library

1. **Queries for Selecting Elements**:
   - **getByText**: Selects elements by visible text.
   - **getByRole**: Selects elements by roles like button, textbox, etc.
   - **getByPlaceholderText**: Selects input fields by their placeholder.
2. **Simulating User Interactions**:
   - Use fireEvent or userEvent to simulate user actions.

Example:

javascript

CopyEdit

```
fireEvent.click(screen.getByText("Submit"));
```

```
fireEvent.change(screen.getByPlaceholderText("Enter name"), {
```

```
target: { value: "John" },
```

```
});
```

Testing Asynchronous Components

DataFetcher.js:

javascript

CopyEdit

```javascript
import React, { useEffect, useState } from "react";

const DataFetcher = ({ fetchData }) => {
  const [data, setData] = useState(null);

  useEffect(() => {
    fetchData().then((response) => setData(response));
  }, [fetchData]);

  if (!data) return <p>Loading...</p>;

  return <p>Data: {data}</p>;
};

export default DataFetcher;
```

DataFetcher.test.js:

javascript

CopyEdit

```
import React from "react";

import { render, screen, waitFor } from "@testing-library/react";

import DataFetcher from "./DataFetcher";


test("fetches and displays data", async () => {

  const mockFetchData = jest.fn().mockResolvedValue("Mock Data");


  render(<DataFetcher fetchData={mockFetchData} />);


  expect(screen.getByText("Loading...")).toBeInTheDocument();


  await waitFor(() => expect(screen.getByText("Data: Mock
Data")).toBeInTheDocument());

});
```

Key Features:

- **mockResolvedValue**: Mocks an asynchronous function that resolves to specific data.
- **waitFor**: Waits for asynchronous updates in the DOM.

186

Best Practices for Testing React Components

1. Test components as users would interact with them, focusing on functionality rather than implementation details.
2. Mock external dependencies like APIs using Jest mocks.
3. Keep tests isolated to ensure they do not depend on the application's state or other tests.
4. Write tests for edge cases (e.g., no data, invalid inputs).

Debugging Common Issues in Full-Stack Development

Debugging is an inevitable part of full-stack development. Here, we'll discuss strategies to debug common issues in both the frontend and backend.

1. Debugging Frontend Issues

Common Issues

1. **Broken User Interface**:
   - Inspect the DOM using browser developer tools.
   - Check for missing or incorrectly applied CSS classes.
2. **Unexpected Behavior**:
   - Add console.log statements to debug the state or props.
   - Use React Developer Tools to inspect component props and state.
3. **API Request Failures**:
   - Check network requests in the browser's Network tab.
   - Verify the request URL, headers, and payload.

Debugging Tools

1. **React Developer Tools**:
   - Inspect React components in the browser.

- ○ Check component hierarchy, state, and props.
2. **Browser Developer Tools**:
    - ○ Use the Elements tab to inspect the DOM.
    - ○ Monitor console logs and network activity.

---

2. Debugging Backend Issues

Common Issues

1. **API Errors**:
    - ○ Check application logs for error messages.
    - ○ Verify the API endpoint and HTTP method.
2. **Database Connection Failures**:
    - ○ Ensure the database service is running.
    - ○ Check connection strings in application.properties.
3. **Unexpected Data**:
    - ○ Use breakpoints or System.out.println to debug method inputs and outputs.

Debugging Tools

1. **Spring Boot Actuator**:
    - ○ Monitor application health, metrics, and logs.

Add the Actuator dependency:

xml

CopyEdit

```xml
<dependency>

  <groupId>org.springframework.boot</groupId>

  <artifactId>spring-boot-starter-actuator</artifactId>

</dependency>
```

2. **IDE Debugger**:
    - ○ Set breakpoints in your code and run the application in debug mode.

　　　　o　Inspect variable values and call stacks during runtime.

---

3. Debugging Frontend-Backend Integration

Common Issues

1. **CORS Errors**:
   - o Ensure the backend allows requests from the frontend's origin.
   - o Use tools like Postman or curl to test APIs independently.
2. **Mismatch in Data Format**:
   - o Verify the structure of API responses matches what the frontend expects.
3. **Authentication Failures**:
   - o Check for missing or invalid tokens in API requests.
   - o Ensure the backend properly validates tokens.

---

4. Logging and Monitoring

Frontend Logging

- Use browser console logs for quick debugging.
- For production, integrate tools like **Sentry** for error tracking.

Backend Logging

- Use Spring Boot's logging framework (Logback by default).

Add logging statements for critical methods:

java

CopyEdit

```
import org.slf4j.Logger;

import org.slf4j.LoggerFactory;
```

```
private static final Logger logger = LoggerFactory.getLogger(MyClass.class);


logger.info("Starting the process...");

logger.error("An error occurred", exception);
```

-

This section explored testing React components using Jest and React Testing Library and strategies for debugging common frontend and backend issues. Effective testing ensures your application functions as expected, while robust debugging practices save time during development.

In the next chapter, we'll cover **Optimizing Performance in Full-Stack Applications**, focusing on frontend performance techniques, backend optimizations, and database tuning.

Chapter 12: Performance Optimization

Optimizing React Applications with Code Splitting and Lazy Loading

Performance optimization is crucial for delivering a smooth and responsive user experience. React applications, especially those with a large codebase, can benefit significantly from techniques like **code splitting** and **lazy loading**, which reduce initial load times and improve perceived performance.

Understanding Code Splitting

Code splitting is the process of breaking your application's code into smaller chunks that are loaded on demand. Instead of sending the entire application to the browser upfront, code splitting enables the browser to load only the code required for the current view or interaction.

Why Use Code Splitting?

1. Reduces the size of the initial JavaScript bundle.
2. Improves page load time and time-to-interactive (TTI).
3. Optimizes performance for users with slower networks or devices.

Implementing Code Splitting with React

React provides built-in support for code splitting through **React.lazy** and **dynamic imports**.

Step 1: Convert Static Imports to Dynamic Imports

Traditionally, you import components like this:

javascript
CopyEdit

import Dashboard from "./components/Dashboard";

With code splitting, use React.lazy to dynamically import the component:

javascript
CopyEdit

```javascript
import React, { Suspense } from "react";

const Dashboard = React.lazy(() => import("./components/Dashboard"));

const App = () => {
  return (
    <div>
      <h1>My App</h1>
      <Suspense fallback={<div>Loading...</div>}>
        <Dashboard />
      </Suspense>
    </div>
  );
};

export default App;
```

Explanation:

1. React.lazy:
    - Dynamically loads the Dashboard component when it is needed.
    - Bundles the component separately during the build process.
2. Suspense:
    - Provides a fallback UI (e.g., a loading spinner) while the component is being loaded.

Step 2: Split Routes for Code Splitting

If your app uses routing, you can split code based on routes.

Before (Without Code Splitting):

javascript
CopyEdit

```javascript
import { BrowserRouter as Router, Route, Routes } from "react-router-dom";
import Home from "./pages/Home";
import About from "./pages/About";

const App = () => {
  return (
    <Router>
      <Routes>
        <Route path="/" element={<Home />} />
        <Route path="/about" element={<About />} />
      </Routes>
    </Router>
  );
};

export default App;
```

After (With Code Splitting):

javascript
CopyEdit

```javascript
import React, { Suspense } from "react";
import { BrowserRouter as Router, Route, Routes } from "react-router-dom";

const Home = React.lazy(() => import("./pages/Home"));
const About = React.lazy(() => import("./pages/About"));
```

193

```
const App = () => {
  return (
    <Router>
      <Suspense fallback={<div>Loading...</div>}>
        <Routes>
          <Route path="/" element={<Home />} />
          <Route path="/about" element={<About />} />
        </Routes>
      </Suspense>
    </Router>
  );
};

export default App;
```

Benefits:

- Only the code for the active route is loaded, reducing the initial bundle size.

Lazy Loading Assets

In addition to components, you can lazy load assets like images or libraries to improve performance.

Lazy Loading Images

Lazy loading images ensures that images are only loaded when they are about to appear in the user's viewport.

Example: Lazy Loading with react-lazy-load-image-component:

Install the library:
bash

npm install react-lazy-load-image-component

1.

Use the LazyLoadImage **component:**

javascript

```
import React from "react";
import { LazyLoadImage } from "react-lazy-load-image-component";

const ImageGallery = () => {
  return (
    <div>
      <h1>Image Gallery</h1>
      <LazyLoadImage
        src="https://example.com/image1.jpg"
        alt="Image 1"
        effect="blur"
      />
      <LazyLoadImage
        src="https://example.com/image2.jpg"
        alt="Image 2"
        effect="blur"
      />
    </div>
  );
};

export default ImageGallery;
```

2. **Features**:
   - effect="blur": Adds a blur effect while the image is loading.
   - Images are loaded only when they are near the viewport.

Lazy Loading Third-Party Libraries

For large third-party libraries, load them only when needed using dynamic imports.

Example: Lazy Loading Lodash:

javascript
CopyEdit
```javascript
import React, { useState } from "react";

const HeavyCalculation = () => {
  const [result, setResult] = useState(null);

  const handleCalculate = async () => {
    const _ = await import("lodash"); // Lazy load lodash
    const numbers = [1, 2, 3, 4, 5];
    setResult(_.sum(numbers));
  };

  return (
    <div>
      <button onClick={handleCalculate}>Calculate Sum</button>
      {result !== null && <p>Sum: {result}</p>}
    </div>
  );
};

export default HeavyCalculation;
```

Benefits:

- Reduces the initial bundle size by loading the library only when it's needed.

Analyzing Bundle Size

After implementing code splitting and lazy loading, analyze your app's bundle size to identify further optimization opportunities.

Tools for Bundle Analysis

1. **Webpack Bundle Analyzer**:

Install the package:
bash
CopyEdit
npm install webpack-bundle-analyzer --save-dev

    ○ Modify package.json:

json
CopyEdit
"scripts": {

"analyze": "react-scripts build && webpack-bundle-analyzer build/static/js/*.js"

}

    ○ Run the analysis:

bash
CopyEdit
npm run analyze

2. **Source Map Explorer**:

Install the package:
bash
CopyEdit
npm install source-map-explorer --save-dev

Analyze the bundle:

bash

CopyEdit

```
npm run build
npx source-map-explorer build/static/js/*.js
```

These tools provide a visual representation of your bundle, highlighting large dependencies and opportunities for optimization.

Best Practices for Code Splitting and Lazy Loading

1. **Split Only Where It Makes Sense**:
   - Code splitting is beneficial for large components or pages. Avoid over-splitting.
2. **Use Fallbacks for Lazy Loading**:
   - Always provide a fallback UI (e.g., a spinner or placeholder) while the component or asset is loading.
3. **Preload Critical Resources**:
   - Use React.Suspense with preloading techniques for resources critical to user interaction.
4. **Avoid Lazy Loading for Critical Components**:
   - Components visible on the initial render (e.g., header, footer) should not be lazy-loaded.

Code splitting and lazy loading are powerful techniques for optimizing React applications. By dynamically loading components, assets, and libraries, you can reduce the initial load time and enhance performance. These techniques ensure that your application delivers a fast and seamless experience for users, especially on slow networks or resource-constrained devices.

In the next section, we'll explore **Optimizing Backend Performance with Spring Boot**, focusing on database tuning, caching, and efficient API design to ensure a performant full-stack application.

Backend Performance Tuning with Caching (e.g., Redis)

Backend performance optimization ensures your application handles requests efficiently, reduces response times, and supports high traffic. One of the most effective techniques is **caching**, which stores frequently accessed data in memory to avoid repetitive computation or database queries.

Understanding Caching

Caching involves storing data in a temporary storage layer (cache) to serve future requests faster. In a typical Spring Boot application, you can use a caching mechanism like **Redis** to reduce database load and improve performance.

Benefits of Caching

1. Reduces database query overhead.
2. Improves response times for frequently accessed data.
3. Scales better under high traffic.

Using Redis for Caching

Redis is a high-performance, in-memory data store that supports key-value caching.

Step 1: Add Redis Dependency

Add the Redis dependency to your pom.xml:

xml

CopyEdit

```
<dependency>
    <groupId>org.springframework.boot</groupId>
    <artifactId>spring-boot-starter-data-redis</artifactId>
```

```
</dependency>
```

Step 2: Configure Redis

In your application.properties, configure the Redis connection:

properties

CopyEdit

```
spring.redis.host=localhost

spring.redis.port=6379
```

Step 3: Enable Caching in Spring Boot

Enable caching in your application:

java

CopyEdit

```
import org.springframework.cache.annotation.EnableCaching;

import org.springframework.context.annotation.Configuration;


@Configuration

@EnableCaching

public class CacheConfig {

}
```

1.
2. Annotate your service methods with @Cacheable, @CacheEvict, or @CachePut as needed.

Step 4: Example Usage

Service Layer:

java

CopyEdit

```java
import org.springframework.cache.annotation.Cacheable;

import org.springframework.stereotype.Service;


@Service

public class ProductService {


    @Cacheable("products")

    public Product getProductById(Long productId) {

        // Simulate a database query

        simulateSlowService();

        return new Product(productId, "Sample Product");

    }


    private void simulateSlowService() {

        try {

            Thread.sleep(3000); // Simulate a slow database query
```

```java
        } catch (InterruptedException e) {

            throw new IllegalStateException(e);

        }

    }

}
```

- **@Cacheable("products")**: Caches the result of the getProductById method. Future calls with the same parameter will return the cached value instead of querying the database.

Controller Layer:

java

CopyEdit

```java
import org.springframework.web.bind.annotation.*;


@RestController
@RequestMapping("/products")
public class ProductController {


    private final ProductService productService;


    public ProductController(ProductService productService) {
        this.productService = productService;
```

```java
}

@GetMapping("/{id}")

public Product getProduct(@PathVariable Long id) {

    return productService.getProductById(id);

}

}
```

Step 5: Clearing the Cache

You can evict cached data using the @CacheEvict annotation. For example:

java

CopyEdit

```java
@CacheEvict(value = "products", allEntries = true)

public void clearCache() {

    // Clears all entries in the 'products' cache

}
```

Best Practices for Caching

1. **Cache Only Frequently Accessed Data**:
   - Avoid caching data that changes often or is seldom requested.

2. **Set Expiration Policies**:
   ○ Use time-to-live (TTL) to ensure stale data is automatically evicted.

properties

CopyEdit

spring.cache.redis.time-to-live=600000 # 10 minutes

3. **Monitor Cache Usage**:
   ○ Use Redis monitoring tools (e.g., redis-cli, RedisInsight) to track cache performance.
4. **Use Cache Key Strategies**:

Define unique cache keys for different use cases:

java

CopyEdit

```
@Cacheable(value = "products", key = "#id + '-' + #locale")

public Product getProduct(Long id, String locale) {

    // Fetch localized product

}
```

Query Optimization in Spring Boot

Inefficient queries are a common bottleneck in backend performance. Optimizing database queries ensures your application handles data-intensive operations efficiently.

Step 1: Write Efficient JPQL and Native Queries

1. **Use Indexed Columns**: Ensure the columns used in WHERE, JOIN, or ORDER BY clauses are indexed in your database schema.

Select Only Required Columns: Instead of fetching entire entities, retrieve only the necessary fields using custom projections:

java

CopyEdit

```
@Query("SELECT new com.example.dto.ProductDTO(p.id, p.name) FROM Product p
WHERE p.category = :category")

List<ProductDTO> findProductsByCategory(@Param("category") String category);
```

2. **Avoid N+1 Query Problems**: Use JOIN FETCH to fetch related entities in a single query:

java

CopyEdit

```
@Query("SELECT p FROM Product p JOIN FETCH p.category WHERE p.id = :id")

Product findProductWithCategory(@Param("id") Long id);
```

Step 2: Leverage Pagination and Sorting

Fetching large datasets can degrade performance. Use pagination to limit results:

java

CopyEdit

```
@Query("SELECT p FROM Product p WHERE p.category = :category")

Page<Product> findProductsByCategory(@Param("category") String category, Pageable
pageable);
```

Controller Example:

java

CopyEdit

```
@GetMapping
```

205

```
public Page<Product> getProducts(@RequestParam int page, @RequestParam int size) {

    return productService.findProducts(PageRequest.of(page, size));

}
```

Step 3: Optimize Relationships in Entities

1. **Lazy vs. Eager Loading**:
   - Use `@OneToMany(fetch = FetchType.LAZY)` to avoid fetching related entities unnecessarily.
2. **Batch Fetching**:

Configure batch size to optimize lazy loading:

properties

CopyEdit

spring.jpa.properties.hibernate.default_batch_fetch_size=10

Step 4: Enable Query Caching

Hibernate provides a second-level cache for query results.

Enable Query Caching:

properties

CopyEdit

spring.jpa.properties.hibernate.cache.use_query_cache=true

spring.jpa.properties.hibernate.cache.region.factory_class=org.hibernate.cache.jcache.JCache
RegionFactory

1. **Mark Queries as Cacheable**:

   java

   CopyEdit

   @Cacheable

   @Query("SELECT p FROM Product p WHERE p.category = :category")

   List<Product> findProductsByCategory(@Param("category") String category);

Step 5: Profile and Analyze Queries

Enable SQL Logging: Log SQL queries to identify slow queries:

properties

CopyEdit

spring.jpa.show-sql=true

spring.jpa.properties.hibernate.format_sql=true

1. **Use Database Tools**:
   - Analyze query performance with tools like **pgAdmin, MySQL Workbench**, or **EXPLAIN ANALYZE**.
2. **JPA Query Performance Tools**:
   - Use **Spring Boot Actuator** or external tools like **New Relic** to monitor database performance in real time.

Best Practices for Query Optimization

1. **Avoid Full Table Scans**:
   - Always use indexed columns in WHERE and JOIN clauses.
2. **Use Prepared Statements**:
   - Avoid concatenating query strings to prevent SQL injection and improve query parsing.
3. **Denormalize When Necessary**:

207

- For performance-critical use cases, consider denormalizing data to reduce complex joins.

4. **Test Queries with Real Data**:
   - Simulate production scenarios to test query performance under realistic loads.

Backend performance can be significantly improved by implementing caching with Redis and optimizing database queries in Spring Boot. Caching reduces load on the database and accelerates response times, while query optimization ensures efficient data retrieval. Together, these techniques help your application scale effectively and handle high traffic.

In the next chapter, we'll explore **Scalability and Monitoring**, focusing on load balancing, application health checks, and tools to monitor application performance.

Chapter 13: Continuous Integration and Deployment

Setting Up CI/CD Pipelines with GitHub Actions

Continuous Integration and Continuous Deployment (CI/CD) pipelines automate the process of building, testing, and deploying your application. **GitHub Actions** is a powerful tool for creating CI/CD pipelines directly within your GitHub repository, making it seamless to integrate testing and deployment workflows.

What is CI/CD?

1. **Continuous Integration (CI)**:
   - Automatically builds and tests code changes as they are pushed to the repository.
   - Ensures that changes integrate smoothly into the codebase.
2. **Continuous Deployment (CD)**:
   - Automatically deploys changes to a staging or production environment once they pass the CI pipeline.

Benefits of CI/CD:

- Detect bugs early.
- Reduce manual deployment overhead.
- Ensure consistent builds and deployments.

Setting Up GitHub Actions for CI/CD

Step 1: Create a GitHub Repository

Push your project to a GitHub repository:

bash

CopyEdit

```
git init
git add .
git commit -m "Initial commit"
git branch -M main
git remote add origin https://github.com/username/repository.git
git push -u origin main
```

1. Navigate to your repository on GitHub.

Step 2: Add a GitHub Actions Workflow

1. In the repository, go to the **Actions** tab.
2. Click **Set up a workflow yourself** or select a predefined workflow template.
3. Create a file named .github/workflows/ci-cd.yml in your repository.

Step 3: Define the Workflow

Here's an example workflow for a full-stack application with a React frontend and a Spring Boot backend:

ci-cd.yml:

yaml
CopyEdit

```
name: CI/CD Pipeline

on:
  push:
    branches:
      - main
  pull_request:
    branches:
      - main
```

```yaml
jobs:
  build:
    name: Build and Test
    runs-on: ubuntu-latest

    steps:
    # Step 1: Checkout the code
    - name: Checkout Code
      uses: actions/checkout@v3

    # Step 2: Set up Java
    - name: Set up JDK 11
      uses: actions/setup-java@v3
      with:
        java-version: 11

    # Step 3: Build Spring Boot Backend
    - name: Build Backend
      run: |
        cd backend
        ./mvnw clean package

    # Step 4: Run Backend Tests
    - name: Run Backend Tests
      run: |
        cd backend
        ./mvnw test

    # Step 5: Set up Node.js
    - name: Set up Node.js
      uses: actions/setup-node@v3
      with:
        node-version: 16
```

```yaml
# Step 6: Build React Frontend
- name: Build Frontend
  run: |
    cd frontend
    npm install
    npm run build

# Step 7: Archive Build Artifacts
- name: Upload Artifacts
  uses: actions/upload-artifact@v3
  with:
    name: build-artifacts
    path: |
      backend/target/app.jar
      frontend/build

deploy:
  name: Deploy to Production
  runs-on: ubuntu-latest
  needs: build
  if: github.ref == 'refs/heads/main'

  steps:
  # Step 1: Checkout the code
  - name: Checkout Code
    uses: actions/checkout@v3

  # Step 2: Deploy Backend
  - name: Deploy Backend
    run: |
      scp -i ~/.ssh/id_rsa backend/target/app.jar user@your-server:/path/to/deployment
      ssh -i ~/.ssh/id_rsa user@your-server "sudo systemctl restart your-app-service"
```

```
# Step 3: Deploy Frontend
- name: Deploy Frontend
  run: |
    scp -i ~/.ssh/id_rsa -r frontend/build/* user@your-server:/path/to/frontend
```

Explanation of the Workflow

1. **Triggers**:
   - The pipeline runs on push or pull_request events targeting the main branch.
2. **Jobs**:
   - **Build**: Builds and tests the backend and frontend.
   - **Deploy**: Deploys the backend and frontend to the production server.
3. **Key Actions**:
   - actions/checkout: Checks out the repository.
   - setup-java: Sets up Java for building the backend.
   - setup-node: Sets up Node.js for building the frontend.
   - upload-artifact: Saves build artifacts for reuse.
   - scp **and** ssh: Deploy the application to the server.

Customizing the Workflow

1. **Environment-Specific Deployments**:

Add conditional logic for deploying to different environments:

yaml

CopyEdit

```
if: github.ref == 'refs/heads/main' # Deploy to production
```

2. **Secrets**:
   - Store sensitive information (e.g., SSH keys, API keys) in GitHub **Secrets**.

213

Access secrets in the workflow:

yaml

CopyEdit

```
- name: Deploy Backend
  env:
    SSH_KEY: ${{ secrets.SSH_KEY }}
  run: |
    echo "$SSH_KEY" > ~/.ssh/id_rsa
    chmod 600 ~/.ssh/id_rsa
```

3. **Matrix Builds**:

Test your application on multiple environments or configurations:

yaml

CopyEdit

```
strategy:
  matrix:
    node-version: [14, 16, 18]
```

Monitoring the Workflow

1. **View Workflow Logs**:
   - Navigate to the **Actions** tab in your GitHub repository.
   - Click on a specific workflow run to view detailed logs.

2. **Fixing Failures**:
   - Use logs to debug build or test failures.
   - Ensure all dependencies are installed and environment variables are correctly configured.

Best Practices for CI/CD Pipelines

1. **Run Tests Early**:
   - Ensure all unit and integration tests are run in the CI pipeline before deployment.

2. **Keep Pipelines Fast**:
   - ○ Parallelize jobs or skip unnecessary steps to reduce pipeline runtime.
3. **Use Separate Environments**:
   - ○ Use staging and production environments to avoid deploying untested changes directly to production.
4. **Monitor Pipeline Health**:
   - ○ Use tools like **GitHub Actions Insights** to monitor pipeline performance and success rates.

Setting up a CI/CD pipeline with GitHub Actions ensures your application is continuously built, tested, and deployed with minimal manual intervention. This approach helps maintain code quality and accelerates the development lifecycle. With automated pipelines, you can focus on building features while ensuring a reliable deployment process.

In the next section, we'll cover **Monitoring and Scaling Full-Stack Applications**, focusing on application health checks, logging, and scaling strategies for handling increased traffic.

Automating Tests and Deployments

Automating tests and deployments in a CI/CD pipeline ensures that every code change is tested, verified, and deployed with minimal manual intervention. This process reduces errors, speeds up delivery, and enhances software reliability.

Automating Tests in CI/CD Pipelines

A well-structured CI/CD pipeline should automatically run tests whenever new code is pushed or merged into the main branch. These tests verify the correctness of both frontend and backend functionality before deployment.

---

1. Types of Automated Tests

1. **Unit Tests**:
   - Verify individual components or methods.
   - Use **JUnit** and **Mockito** for Spring Boot.
   - Use **Jest** and **React Testing Library** for React.
2. **Integration Tests**:
   - Ensure that different modules work together.
   - Use **Spring Boot Test** for backend testing.
3. **End-to-End (E2E) Tests**:
   - Test the complete user workflow.
   - Use **Cypress** or **Selenium** for frontend-backend testing.
4. **Performance and Security Tests**:
   - Run API load tests using **JMeter**.
   - Use **OWASP ZAP** for security testing.

---

2. Implementing Automated Tests in a GitHub Actions CI Pipeline

.github/workflows/ci.yml:

yaml

CopyEdit

```
name: CI with Automated Tests


on:
  push:
    branches:
      - main
  pull_request:
```

```yaml
    branches:
      - main

jobs:
  test:
    name: Run Automated Tests
    runs-on: ubuntu-latest

    steps:
      # Step 1: Checkout Code
      - name: Checkout Code
        uses: actions/checkout@v3

      # Step 2: Set up Java
      - name: Set up Java
        uses: actions/setup-java@v3
        with:
          java-version: 11

      # Step 3: Run Spring Boot Tests
      - name: Run Backend Tests
```

```
run: |

  cd backend

  ./mvnw test


# Step 4: Set up Node.js

- name: Set up Node.js

  uses: actions/setup-node@v3

  with:

    node-version: 16


# Step 5: Run Frontend Tests

- name: Run Frontend Tests

  run: |

    cd frontend

    npm install

    npm test
```

Automating Deployments

After successful tests, the pipeline should automatically deploy the application.

1. Deploying Spring Boot Backend to AWS/GCP

Modify the CI/CD workflow to include deployment steps.

Example Deployment Pipeline (deploy.yml):

yaml

CopyEdit

```
name: Deploy to Server

on:
  push:
    branches:
      - main

jobs:
  deploy:
    runs-on: ubuntu-latest
    needs: test

    steps:
      - name: Checkout Code
        uses: actions/checkout@v3

      - name: Deploy Backend
```

```
run: |

  scp -i ~/.ssh/id_rsa backend/target/app.jar user@server-ip:/path/to/deployment

  ssh -i ~/.ssh/id_rsa user@server-ip "sudo systemctl restart your-app-service"


- name: Deploy Frontend

  run: |

    scp -i ~/.ssh/id_rsa -r frontend/build/* user@server-ip:/var/www/html
```

Best Practices for Automated Testing and Deployment

1. **Run Tests on Every Commit**: Prevent breaking changes from reaching production.
2. **Use Staging Environments**: Deploy to staging before production.
3. **Monitor Deployments**: Use logs and monitoring tools to detect issues post-deployment.
4. **Rollback on Failure**: Automate rollbacks for failed deployments.

Monitoring Applications in Production with Spring Boot Actuator

Once your application is deployed, monitoring its health and performance is crucial. **Spring Boot Actuator** provides built-in endpoints to monitor application metrics, health status, and logs.

---

1. Enabling Spring Boot Actuator

Step 1: Add Actuator Dependency

Add the following dependency to your pom.xml:

xml

CopyEdit

```xml
<dependency>

    <groupId>org.springframework.boot</groupId>

    <artifactId>spring-boot-starter-actuator</artifactId>

</dependency>
```

Step 2: Configure Actuator Endpoints

In application.properties:

properties

CopyEdit

```properties
management.endpoints.web.exposure.include=*

management.endpoint.health.show-details=always

management.endpoint.metrics.enabled=true
```

Step 3: Access Actuator Endpoints

Start your Spring Boot application and visit:

- **Health check:** http://localhost:8080/actuator/health
- **Metrics:** http://localhost:8080/actuator/metrics

- Application info: http://localhost:8080/actuator/info

2. Common Actuator Endpoints

Endpoint	Description
/actuator/health	Displays the health status of the application.
/actuator/info	Provides application details.
/actuator/metrics	Shows performance metrics (CPU, memory usage).
/actuator/loggers	Adjusts logging levels dynamically.

---

3. Integrating Actuator with Prometheus and Grafana for Monitoring

Actuator metrics can be exported to **Prometheus**, a powerful monitoring tool, and visualized in **Grafana**.

Step 1: Add Prometheus Dependency

xml

CopyEdit

```xml
<dependency>

    <groupId>io.micrometer</groupId>

    <artifactId>micrometer-registry-prometheus</artifactId>

</dependency>
```

Step 2: Enable Prometheus Metrics

Add this to application.properties:

properties

CopyEdit

management.metrics.export.prometheus.enabled=true

management.endpoints.web.exposure.include=health,metrics,prometheus

Step 3: Set Up Prometheus

Install Prometheus:

bash

CopyEdit

sudo apt install prometheus

1. Edit the Prometheus config (prometheus.yml):

   yaml

   CopyEdit

   scrape_configs:

   - job_name: 'spring-boot-app'

     metrics_path: '/actuator/prometheus'

     static_configs:

       - targets: ['localhost:8080']

2. Start Prometheus:

   bash

   CopyEdit

   prometheus --config.file=prometheus.yml

---

4. Setting Up Grafana for Visualization

Install Grafana:

bash

CopyEdit

sudo apt install grafana

1. Access Grafana at http://localhost:3000.
2. Add **Prometheus** as a data source.
3. Create dashboards to visualize application health, latency, and database queries.

---

5. Using Log Aggregation with ELK Stack (Elasticsearch, Logstash, Kibana)

For centralized logging, integrate your Spring Boot logs with ELK.

Install Filebeat:

bash

CopyEdit

sudo apt install filebeat

1. **Configure Filebeat** to send logs to **Elasticsearch**.
2. **Visualize logs in Kibana** for real-time monitoring.

Best Practices for Monitoring

1. **Set Up Alerts**:
    o Configure alerts in Grafana to notify about downtime.
    o Example: Send an email when CPU usage exceeds 80%.
2. **Monitor Database Queries**:

Enable Hibernate statistics:

properties

CopyEdit

spring.jpa.properties.hibernate.generate_statistics=true

3. **Track API Latency**:
   - Use Actuator metrics to detect slow endpoints.
4. **Log Errors and Warnings**:
   - Store logs in **Elasticsearch** for future analysis.

By automating tests and deployments, you ensure that your application remains reliable and error-free. **Spring Boot Actuator** helps monitor application health, while **Prometheus, Grafana**, and **ELK** provide deep insights into performance and logging. Implementing these tools ensures a smooth-running production system with minimal downtime.

In the next chapter, we'll explore **Scaling and Load Balancing Full-Stack Applications**, focusing on horizontal scaling, load balancers, and optimizing for high traffic environments.

Chapter 14: Real-World Project 1 – E-Commerce Application

Building the Backend for Products, Cart, and Orders

In this chapter, we will build the backend of a **full-stack e-commerce application** using **Spring Boot**. The backend will handle **product management, shopping cart functionality, and order processing**. It will expose REST APIs that the frontend (React) will consume.

Backend Features

1. **Product Management**:
    - CRUD operations for products (Create, Read, Update, Delete).
    - Category and price filtering.
2. **Shopping Cart**:
    - Add/remove products from the cart.
    - Persist the cart for authenticated users.
3. **Order Processing**:
    - Checkout and place orders.
    - Track order status.

Step 1: Setting Up the Spring Boot Project

1.1 Initialize Spring Boot Application

Use **Spring Initializr** or create a project manually with the following dependencies:

xml

CopyEdit

```
<dependencies>
  <!-- Spring Web for REST APIs -->
```

```xml
<dependency>
    <groupId>org.springframework.boot</groupId>
    <artifactId>spring-boot-starter-web</artifactId>
</dependency>

<!-- Spring Data JPA for Database Access -->
<dependency>
    <groupId>org.springframework.boot</groupId>
    <artifactId>spring-boot-starter-data-jpa</artifactId>
</dependency>

<!-- H2 Database for Development (Switch to MySQL for Production) -->
<dependency>
    <groupId>com.h2database</groupId>
    <artifactId>h2</artifactId>
    <scope>runtime</scope>
</dependency>

<!-- Spring Security for User Authentication -->
<dependency>
    <groupId>org.springframework.boot</groupId>
    <artifactId>spring-boot-starter-security</artifactId>
</dependency>

<!-- JWT for Secure API Access -->
<dependency>
    <groupId>io.jsonwebtoken</groupId>
    <artifactId>jjwt</artifactId>
    <version>0.11.2</version>
</dependency>
</dependencies>
```

1.2 Configure Database in application.properties

For **development**, use an in-memory H2 database:

properties
CopyEdit

```
spring.datasource.url=jdbc:h2:mem:ecommerce
spring.datasource.driverClassName=org.h2.Driver
spring.datasource.username=sa
spring.datasource.password=
spring.jpa.database-platform=org.hibernate.dialect.H2Dialect
spring.h2.console.enabled=true
```

For **production**, switch to MySQL or PostgreSQL.

Step 2: Creating the Product Entity and API

2.1 Define the Product Entity

java
CopyEdit

```java
package com.ecommerce.model;

import jakarta.persistence.*;
import lombok.*;

@Entity
@Getter @Setter @NoArgsConstructor @AllArgsConstructor
public class Product {

    @Id
    @GeneratedValue(strategy = GenerationType.IDENTITY)
    private Long id;
    private String name;
```

```
    private String description;
    private double price;
    private String category;
    private String imageUrl;
}
```

2.2 Create the ProductRepository

java

CopyEdit

```
package com.ecommerce.repository;

import com.ecommerce.model.Product;
import org.springframework.data.jpa.repository.JpaRepository;
import java.util.List;

public interface ProductRepository extends JpaRepository<Product, Long> {
    List<Product> findByCategory(String category);
}
```

2.3 Create the ProductService

java

CopyEdit

```
package com.ecommerce.service;

import com.ecommerce.model.Product;
import com.ecommerce.repository.ProductRepository;
import org.springframework.stereotype.Service;
import java.util.List;

@Service
```

229

```java
public class ProductService {

    private final ProductRepository productRepository;

    public ProductService(ProductRepository productRepository) {
        this.productRepository = productRepository;
    }

    public List<Product> getAllProducts() {
        return productRepository.findAll();
    }

    public Product getProductById(Long id) {
        return productRepository.findById(id).orElse(null);
    }

    public List<Product> getProductsByCategory(String category) {
        return productRepository.findByCategory(category);
    }

    public Product addProduct(Product product) {
        return productRepository.save(product);
    }

    public Product updateProduct(Long id, Product productDetails) {
        Product product = productRepository.findById(id).orElse(null);
        if (product != null) {
            product.setName(productDetails.getName());
            product.setDescription(productDetails.getDescription());
            product.setPrice(productDetails.getPrice());
            product.setCategory(productDetails.getCategory());
            product.setImageUrl(productDetails.getImageUrl());
            return productRepository.save(product);
        }
```

```java
        return null;
    }

    public void deleteProduct(Long id) {
        productRepository.deleteById(id);
    }
}
```

2.4 Create the ProductController

java

CopyEdit

```java
package com.ecommerce.controller;

import com.ecommerce.model.Product;
import com.ecommerce.service.ProductService;
import org.springframework.web.bind.annotation.*;

import java.util.List;

@RestController
@RequestMapping("/api/products")
public class ProductController {

    private final ProductService productService;

    public ProductController(ProductService productService) {
        this.productService = productService;
    }

    @GetMapping
    public List<Product> getAllProducts() {
        return productService.getAllProducts();
```

```
    }

    @GetMapping("/{id}")
    public Product getProductById(@PathVariable Long id) {
        return productService.getProductById(id);
    }

    @GetMapping("/category/{category}")
    public List<Product> getProductsByCategory(@PathVariable String category) {
        return productService.getProductsByCategory(category);
    }

    @PostMapping
    public Product addProduct(@RequestBody Product product) {
        return productService.addProduct(product);
    }

    @PutMapping("/{id}")
    public Product updateProduct(@PathVariable Long id, @RequestBody Product product) {
        return productService.updateProduct(id, product);
    }

    @DeleteMapping("/{id}")
    public void deleteProduct(@PathVariable Long id) {
        productService.deleteProduct(id);
    }
}
```

Step 3: Creating the Shopping Cart Functionality

3.1 Define the CartItem Entity

java

CopyEdit

```java
package com.ecommerce.model;

import jakarta.persistence.*;
import lombok.*;

@Entity
@Getter @Setter @NoArgsConstructor @AllArgsConstructor
public class CartItem {

    @Id
    @GeneratedValue(strategy = GenerationType.IDENTITY)
    private Long id;

    @ManyToOne
    private Product product;

    private int quantity;
}
```

3.2 Create the CartService

java

CopyEdit

```java
package com.ecommerce.service;

import com.ecommerce.model.CartItem;
import com.ecommerce.repository.CartItemRepository;
import org.springframework.stereotype.Service;
import java.util.List;
```

233

```java
@Service
public class CartService {

    private final CartItemRepository cartRepository;

    public CartService(CartItemRepository cartRepository) {
        this.cartRepository = cartRepository;
    }

    public List<CartItem> getCartItems() {
        return cartRepository.findAll();
    }

    public CartItem addToCart(CartItem cartItem) {
        return cartRepository.save(cartItem);
    }

    public void removeFromCart(Long id) {
        cartRepository.deleteById(id);
    }
}
```

3.3 Create the CartController

java

CopyEdit

```java
package com.ecommerce.controller;

import com.ecommerce.model.CartItem;
import com.ecommerce.service.CartService;
import org.springframework.web.bind.annotation.*;
```

```java
import java.util.List;

@RestController
@RequestMapping("/api/cart")
public class CartController {

    private final CartService cartService;

    public CartController(CartService cartService) {
        this.cartService = cartService;
    }

    @GetMapping
    public List<CartItem> getCartItems() {
        return cartService.getCartItems();
    }

    @PostMapping
    public CartItem addToCart(@RequestBody CartItem cartItem) {
        return cartService.addToCart(cartItem);
    }

    @DeleteMapping("/{id}")
    public void removeFromCart(@PathVariable Long id) {
        cartService.removeFromCart(id);
    }
}
```

Next Steps

- Implement **Order Processing** (Checkout, Payments, Order History).
- Integrate **JWT Authentication** for secure API access.

- Implement **Database Optimization & Caching** for performance.

We have built the foundational backend for an e-commerce application, covering product management, shopping cart functionality, and REST APIs. In the next section, we will add **Order Processing and User Authentication**, followed by integrating this backend with a React frontend.

Creating a User-Friendly Frontend Shopping Interface

Now that we have built the backend for our **e-commerce application**, we will create a **React frontend** to allow users to browse products, manage their shopping cart, and place orders.

Step 1: Setting Up the React Frontend

1.1 Initialize React App

Run the following command to create a new React project:

bash

CopyEdit

```
npx create-react-app ecommerce-frontend

cd ecommerce-frontend

npm install axios react-router-dom redux react-redux redux-thunk @mui/material @emotion/react @emotion/styled
```

- **axios**: For making API requests.
- **react-router-dom**: For navigation.
- **redux, react-redux, redux-thunk**: For state management.
- **@mui/material**: For UI components.

Step 2: Structuring the Frontend

Create the following folder structure inside src/:

css

CopyEdit

src/

|── components/

| ├── ProductList.js

| ├── ProductCard.js

| ├── Cart.js

|── pages/

| ├── Home.js

| ├── ProductDetail.js

| ├── Checkout.js

|── redux/

| ├── store.js

| ├── actions/

| ├── reducers/

|── App.js

|── index.js

Step 3: Fetching Products from the Backend

3.1 Create the API Service

Create a file src/api.js to centralize API calls:

javascript

CopyEdit

```javascript
import axios from "axios";


const API_BASE_URL = "http://localhost:8080/api";


export const fetchProducts = async () => {

  const response = await axios.get(`${API_BASE_URL}/products`);

  return response.data;

};


export const fetchProductById = async (id) => {

  const response = await axios.get(`${API_BASE_URL}/products/${id}`);

  return response.data;

};
```

3.2 Create the ProductList Component

src/components/ProductList.js:

javascript

CopyEdit

```javascript
import React, { useEffect, useState } from "react";

import { fetchProducts } from "../api";

import ProductCard from "./ProductCard";

import { Grid } from "@mui/material";


const ProductList = () => {

  const [products, setProducts] = useState([]);


  useEffect(() => {

    fetchProducts().then(setProducts);

  }, []);


  return (

    <Grid container spacing={2}>

      {products.map((product) => (

        <Grid item key={product.id} xs={12} sm={6} md={4}>

          <ProductCard product={product} />
```

```
        </Grid>

      ))}

    </Grid>

  );

};


export default ProductList;
```

3.3 Create the ProductCard Component

src/components/ProductCard.js:

javascript

CopyEdit

```
import React from "react";

import { Card, CardMedia, CardContent, Typography, Button } from "@mui/material";

import { useNavigate } from "react-router-dom";


const ProductCard = ({ product }) => {

  const navigate = useNavigate();


  return (

    <Card>
```

```jsx
    <CardMedia component="img" height="140" image={product.imageUrl}
alt={product.name} />

      <CardContent>

        <Typography variant="h6">{product.name}</Typography>

        <Typography variant="body2">${product.price}</Typography>

        <Button onClick={() => navigate(`/product/${product.id}`)}>View
Details</Button>

      </CardContent>

    </Card>

  );

};


export default ProductCard;
```

Step 4: Implementing Shopping Cart Functionality

4.1 Create Redux Store

src/redux/store.js:

javascript

CopyEdit

```javascript
import { createStore, applyMiddleware, combineReducers } from "redux";

import thunk from "redux-thunk";
```

```javascript
import cartReducer from "./reducers/cartReducer";

const rootReducer = combineReducers({
  cart: cartReducer,
});

const store = createStore(rootReducer, applyMiddleware(thunk));

export default store;
```

4.2 Create Cart Reducer and Actions

src/redux/reducers/cartReducer.js:

javascript

CopyEdit

```javascript
const initialState = {
  cartItems: [],
};

const cartReducer = (state = initialState, action) => {
  switch (action.type) {
```

```javascript
    case "ADD_TO_CART":

        return { ...state, cartItems: [...state.cartItems, action.payload] };

    case "REMOVE_FROM_CART":

        return { ...state, cartItems: state.cartItems.filter(item => item.id !== action.payload) };

    default:

        return state;

  }

};


export default cartReducer;
```

src/redux/actions/cartActions.js:

javascript

CopyEdit

```javascript
export const addToCart = (product) => ({

  type: "ADD_TO_CART",

  payload: product,

});


export const removeFromCart = (id) => ({

  type: "REMOVE_FROM_CART",
```

```
  payload: id,

});
```

4.3 Create the Cart Component

src/components/Cart.js:

javascript

CopyEdit

```javascript
import React from "react";

import { useSelector, useDispatch } from "react-redux";

import { removeFromCart } from "../redux/actions/cartActions";

import { Button, Typography } from "@mui/material";


const Cart = () => {

  const cartItems = useSelector((state) => state.cart.cartItems);

  const dispatch = useDispatch();


  return (

    <div>

      <Typography variant="h5">Shopping Cart</Typography>

      {cartItems.map((item) => (
```

```jsx
          <div key={item.id}>

            <Typography>{item.name} - ${item.price}</Typography>

            <Button onClick={() =>
dispatch(removeFromCart(item.id))}>Remove</Button>

          </div>

        ))}

      </div>

    );

};


export default Cart;
```

Step 5: Routing and Navigation

Modify src/App.js to include routing:

javascript

CopyEdit

```javascript
import React from "react";

import { BrowserRouter as Router, Route, Routes } from "react-router-dom";

import ProductList from "./components/ProductList";

import Cart from "./components/Cart";
```

245

```
const App = () => {

  return (

    <Router>

      <Routes>

        <Route path="/" element={<ProductList />} />

        <Route path="/cart" element={<Cart />} />

      </Routes>

    </Router>

  );

};


export default App;
```

Deploying the Application to the Cloud

Now that our application is ready, we can deploy it using **AWS, GCP, or DigitalOcean**.

Step 1: Deploying the Backend (Spring Boot)

1.1 Package and Upload to Server

bash

CopyEdit

```
mvn clean package

scp target/app.jar user@server-ip:/home/user

ssh user@server-ip "java -jar /home/user/app.jar"
```

Step 2: Deploying the Frontend (React)

2.1 Build the React App

bash

CopyEdit

```
npm run build
```

2.2 Upload to Nginx

bash

CopyEdit

```
scp -r build/* user@server-ip:/var/www/html
```

2.3 Configure Nginx

nginx

```
server {

    listen 80;

    root /var/www/html;

    index index.html;

    location / {

        try_files $uri /index.html;

    }


    location /api/ {

        proxy_pass http://localhost:8080;

    }

}
```

Restart Nginx:

bash

```
sudo systemctl restart nginx
```

In this chapter, we built a **full-stack e-commerce application**, covering: ■ **Spring Boot backend** with products, cart, and orders.

248

- **React frontend** for user-friendly shopping.
- **Redux state management** for the cart.
- **Cloud deployment** with Nginx and Spring Boot.

In the next chapter, we will extend the application by adding **authentication (JWT, OAuth2), order history, and payment integration (Stripe, PayPal).**

Chapter 15: Real-World Project 2 – Blog Platform

Developing REST APIs for Posts, Comments, and User Management

In this chapter, we will build the **backend for a Blog Platform** using **Spring Boot**. This backend will provide REST APIs to manage:

- **Posts**: Create, read, update, delete blog posts.
- **Comments**: Allow users to comment on posts.
- **User Management**: Implement authentication and role-based access control.

Step 1: Setting Up the Spring Boot Project

1.1 Initialize the Spring Boot Application

Use **Spring Initializr** or create a project manually with the following dependencies:

xml

CopyEdit

```
<dependencies>
    <!-- Spring Web for REST APIs -->
    <dependency>
        <groupId>org.springframework.boot</groupId>
        <artifactId>spring-boot-starter-web</artifactId>
    </dependency>

    <!-- Spring Data JPA for Database Access -->
    <dependency>
        <groupId>org.springframework.boot</groupId>
        <artifactId>spring-boot-starter-data-jpa</artifactId>
```

```xml
        </dependency>

        <!-- H2 Database for Development -->
        <dependency>
            <groupId>com.h2database</groupId>
            <artifactId>h2</artifactId>
            <scope>runtime</scope>
        </dependency>

        <!-- Spring Security for Authentication -->
        <dependency>
            <groupId>org.springframework.boot</groupId>
            <artifactId>spring-boot-starter-security</artifactId>
        </dependency>

        <!-- JWT for Secure API Access -->
        <dependency>
            <groupId>io.jsonwebtoken</groupId>
            <artifactId>jjwt</artifactId>
            <version>0.11.2</version>
        </dependency>
    </dependencies>
```

1.2 Configure Database in application.properties

For **development,** use an in-memory H2 database:

properties
CopyEdit

```properties
spring.datasource.url=jdbc:h2:mem:blogdb
spring.datasource.driverClassName=org.h2.Driver
spring.datasource.username=sa
spring.datasource.password=
```

```
spring.jpa.database-platform=org.hibernate.dialect.H2Dialect
spring.h2.console.enabled=true
```

For **production**, switch to MySQL or PostgreSQL.

Step 2: Building the Blog Post API

2.1 Define the Post Entity

java
CopyEdit
```java
package com.blog.model;

import jakarta.persistence.*;
import lombok.*;

import java.time.LocalDateTime;
import java.util.List;

@Entity
@Getter @Setter @NoArgsConstructor @AllArgsConstructor
public class Post {

    @Id
    @GeneratedValue(strategy = GenerationType.IDENTITY)
    private Long id;

    private String title;
    private String content;

    @ManyToOne
    private User author;
```

```java
private LocalDateTime createdAt = LocalDateTime.now();

@OneToMany(mappedBy = "post", cascade = CascadeType.ALL, orphanRemoval = true)
private List<Comment> comments;
}
```

2.2 Create the PostRepository

java

CopyEdit

```java
package com.blog.repository;

import com.blog.model.Post;
import org.springframework.data.jpa.repository.JpaRepository;
import java.util.List;

public interface PostRepository extends JpaRepository<Post, Long> {
    List<Post> findByAuthorId(Long authorId);
}
```

2.3 Implement the PostService

java

CopyEdit

```java
package com.blog.service;

import com.blog.model.Post;
import com.blog.repository.PostRepository;
import org.springframework.stereotype.Service;
import java.util.List;

@Service
```

```java
public class PostService {

    private final PostRepository postRepository;

    public PostService(PostRepository postRepository) {
        this.postRepository = postRepository;
    }

    public List<Post> getAllPosts() {
        return postRepository.findAll();
    }

    public Post getPostById(Long id) {
        return postRepository.findById(id).orElse(null);
    }

    public Post createPost(Post post) {
        return postRepository.save(post);
    }

    public void deletePost(Long id) {
        postRepository.deleteById(id);
    }
}
```

2.4 Create the PostController

java

CopyEdit

```java
package com.blog.controller;

import com.blog.model.Post;
import com.blog.service.PostService;
```

```java
import org.springframework.web.bind.annotation.*;

import java.util.List;

@RestController
@RequestMapping("/api/posts")
public class PostController {

    private final PostService postService;

    public PostController(PostService postService) {
        this.postService = postService;
    }

    @GetMapping
    public List<Post> getAllPosts() {
        return postService.getAllPosts();
    }

    @GetMapping("/{id}")
    public Post getPostById(@PathVariable Long id) {
        return postService.getPostById(id);
    }

    @PostMapping
    public Post createPost(@RequestBody Post post) {
        return postService.createPost(post);
    }

    @DeleteMapping("/{id}")
    public void deletePost(@PathVariable Long id) {
        postService.deletePost(id);
    }
}
```

Step 3: Implementing Comments API

3.1 Define the Comment Entity

java

CopyEdit

```java
package com.blog.model;

import jakarta.persistence.*;
import lombok.*;

import java.time.LocalDateTime;

@Entity
@Getter @Setter @NoArgsConstructor @AllArgsConstructor
public class Comment {

    @Id
    @GeneratedValue(strategy = GenerationType.IDENTITY)
    private Long id;

    private String content;

    @ManyToOne
    private Post post;

    @ManyToOne
    private User author;

    private LocalDateTime createdAt = LocalDateTime.now();
}
```

3.2 Create the CommentRepository

java

CopyEdit

```java
package com.blog.repository;

import com.blog.model.Comment;
import org.springframework.data.jpa.repository.JpaRepository;
import java.util.List;

public interface CommentRepository extends JpaRepository<Comment, Long> {
    List<Comment> findByPostId(Long postId);
}
```

3.3 Implement the CommentService

java

CopyEdit

```java
package com.blog.service;

import com.blog.model.Comment;
import com.blog.repository.CommentRepository;
import org.springframework.stereotype.Service;
import java.util.List;

@Service
public class CommentService {

    private final CommentRepository commentRepository;

    public CommentService(CommentRepository commentRepository) {
        this.commentRepository = commentRepository;
```

257

```java
    }

    public List<Comment> getCommentsByPost(Long postId) {
        return commentRepository.findByPostId(postId);
    }

    public Comment addComment(Comment comment) {
        return commentRepository.save(comment);
    }

    public void deleteComment(Long id) {
        commentRepository.deleteById(id);
    }
}
```

3.4 Create the CommentController

java

CopyEdit

```java
package com.blog.controller;

import com.blog.model.Comment;
import com.blog.service.CommentService;
import org.springframework.web.bind.annotation.*;

import java.util.List;

@RestController
@RequestMapping("/api/comments")
public class CommentController {

    private final CommentService commentService;
```

```
public CommentController(CommentService commentService) {
    this.commentService = commentService;
}

@GetMapping("/post/{postId}")
public List<Comment> getCommentsByPost(@PathVariable Long postId) {
    return commentService.getCommentsByPost(postId);
}

@PostMapping
public Comment addComment(@RequestBody Comment comment) {
    return commentService.addComment(comment);
}

@DeleteMapping("/{id}")
public void deleteComment(@PathVariable Long id) {
    commentService.deleteComment(id);
}
}
```

Next Steps

- Implement **User Management (JWT Authentication, Role-Based Access Control).**
- Add **Pagination and Sorting** for posts and comments.
- Optimize performance with **caching and database indexing**.
- Deploy the backend to a **cloud platform (AWS/GCP)**.

We have built the **backend for a blog platform**, covering: ■ **Post Management** (Create, Read, Delete).

■ **Comment System** (Allowing users to engage with blog posts).

■ **RESTful API Design** for integration with a React frontend.

In the next section, we will implement **User Authentication and Authorization**, ensuring that only authorized users can create, edit, or delete posts and comments.

Designing Dynamic Blog Pages in React

Now that we have a **Spring Boot backend** with REST APIs for posts, comments, and user management, it's time to build a **dynamic React frontend**. The goal is to create a modern **blogging interface** where users can:

- Browse and search for blog posts.
- View individual blog posts with comments.
- Create new blog posts (for authenticated users).
- Enhance the UI for responsiveness and accessibility.

Step 1: Setting Up the React Frontend

1.1 Initialize the React App

bash

CopyEdit

```
npx create-react-app blog-frontend

cd blog-frontend

npm install axios react-router-dom redux react-redux redux-thunk @mui/material
@emotion/react @emotion/styled react-quill react-helmet
```

- **axios** → API requests
- **react-router-dom** → Routing
- **redux, react-redux, redux-thunk** → State management
- **@mui/material** → UI components
- **react-quill** → Rich text editor for post creation
- **react-helmet** → SEO optimization

Step 2: Structuring the Frontend

Create the following **folder structure** inside src/:

css

CopyEdit

```
src/
|── components/
|   ├── PostList.js
|   ├── PostCard.js
|   ├── PostDetail.js
|   ├── CreatePost.js
|── pages/
|   ├── Home.js
|   ├── BlogPost.js
|── redux/
|   ├── store.js
|   ├── actions/
|   ├── reducers/
|── App.js
|── index.js
```

Step 3: Fetching and Displaying Blog Posts

3.1 Create API Service

Create src/api.js:

javascript

CopyEdit

```
import axios from "axios";


const API_BASE_URL = "http://localhost:8080/api";


export const fetchPosts = async () => {

  const response = await axios.get(`${API_BASE_URL}/posts`);

  return response.data;

};


export const fetchPostById = async (id) => {

  const response = await axios.get(`${API_BASE_URL}/posts/${id}`);

  return response.data;

};


export const createPost = async (post) => {
```

```javascript
  return axios.post(`${API_BASE_URL}/posts`, post);
};
```

3.2 Create PostList Component

src/components/PostList.js:

javascript

CopyEdit

```javascript
import React, { useEffect, useState } from "react";

import { fetchPosts } from "../api";

import PostCard from "./PostCard";

import { Grid, Container, Typography } from "@mui/material";


const PostList = () => {

  const [posts, setPosts] = useState([]);


  useEffect(() => {

    fetchPosts().then(setPosts);

  }, []);


  return (

    <Container>
```

263

```
        <Typography variant="h4" gutterBottom>Recent Posts</Typography>

        <Grid container spacing={2}>

          {posts.map((post) => (

            <Grid item key={post.id} xs={12} sm={6} md={4}>

              <PostCard post={post} />

            </Grid>

          ))}

        </Grid>

      </Container>

    );

};


export default PostList;
```

_____

3.3 Create PostCard Component

src/components/PostCard.js:

javascript

CopyEdit

```
import React from "react";

import { Card, CardContent, Typography, Button } from "@mui/material";
```

```
import { useNavigate } from "react-router-dom";


const PostCard = ({ post }) => {

  const navigate = useNavigate();


  return (

    <Card>

      <CardContent>

        <Typography variant="h6">{post.title}</Typography>

        <Typography variant="body2">{post.content.substring(0, 100)}...</Typography>

        <Button onClick={() => navigate(`/post/${post.id}`)}>Read More</Button>

      </CardContent>

    </Card>

  );

};


export default PostCard;
```

3.4 Create PostDetail Component

src/components/PostDetail.js:

javascript

CopyEdit

```javascript
import React, { useEffect, useState } from "react";

import { useParams } from "react-router-dom";

import { fetchPostById } from "../api";

import { Container, Typography } from "@mui/material";


const PostDetail = () => {

  const { id } = useParams();

  const [post, setPost] = useState(null);


  useEffect(() => {

    fetchPostById(id).then(setPost);

  }, [id]);


  if (!post) return <p>Loading...</p>;


  return (

    <Container>
```

```
<Typography variant="h3">{post.title}</Typography>

<Typography variant="body1">{post.content}</Typography>

</Container>

);

};


export default PostDetail;
```

Step 4: Creating Blog Posts

4.1 Create CreatePost Component

src/components/CreatePost.js:

javascript

CopyEdit

```
import React, { useState } from "react";

import { createPost } from "../api";

import { Container, TextField, Button } from "@mui/material";

import { useNavigate } from "react-router-dom";

import ReactQuill from "react-quill";

import "react-quill/dist/quill.snow.css";
```

```
const CreatePost = () => {

  const [title, setTitle] = useState("");

  const [content, setContent] = useState("");

  const navigate = useNavigate();


  const handleSubmit = async (e) => {

    e.preventDefault();

    await createPost({ title, content });

    navigate("/");

  };


  return (

    <Container>

      <h2>Create New Post</h2>

      <TextField fullWidth label="Title" value={title} onChange={(e) =>
setTitle(e.target.value)} />

      <ReactQuill value={content} onChange={setContent} />

      <Button variant="contained" onClick={handleSubmit}>Publish</Button>

    </Container>

  );

};
```

export default CreatePost;

Step 5: Setting Up Routing

Modify src/App.js:

javascript

CopyEdit

import React from "react";

import { BrowserRouter as Router, Route, Routes } from "react-router-dom";

import PostList from "./components/PostList";

import PostDetail from "./components/PostDetail";

import CreatePost from "./components/CreatePost";

const App = () => {

  return (

    <Router>

      <Routes>

        <Route path="/" element={<PostList />} />

        <Route path="/post/:id" element={<PostDetail />} />

        <Route path="/create" element={<CreatePost />} />

      </Routes>

269

```
    </Router>

  );

};


export default App;
```

Enhancing SEO and Social Media Integration

1. Using react-helmet for SEO

Install react-helmet:

bash

CopyEdit

```
npm install react-helmet
```


Modify PostDetail.js:

javascript

CopyEdit

```
import { Helmet } from "react-helmet";


const PostDetail = () => {

  // Fetch post data...
```

```
return (

  <>

    <Helmet>

      <title>{post.title} | My Blog</title>

      <meta name="description" content={post.content.substring(0, 150)} />

      <meta property="og:title" content={post.title} />

      <meta property="og:description" content={post.content.substring(0, 150)} />

    </Helmet>

    <Container>

      <Typography variant="h3">{post.title}</Typography>

      <Typography variant="body1">{post.content}</Typography>

    </Container>

  </>

);

};
```

■ **React Blog Frontend Features:**

- **Dynamic Blog·Pages** with routing and state management.
- **Rich Text Editor** for writing posts.
- **SEO Optimization** with react-helmet.

■ **Next Steps**

- **Implement Authentication** (JWT + Role-Based Access).
- **Enable Comments** with a comment form.
- **Deploy to Cloud** (AWS, GCP, Vercel).

In the next chapter, we will **secure user authentication and role-based access**, ensuring only authorized users can create, edit, or delete blog posts.

Chapter 16: Real-World Project 3 – Social Media Dashboard

Implementing Real-Time Notifications and Messaging

A **Social Media Dashboard** requires real-time features like **notifications and messaging**. In this chapter, we will build the **backend using Spring Boot** and the **frontend using React**, integrating **WebSockets** for real-time updates.

Step 1: Setting Up the Backend with Spring Boot

1.1 Initialize Spring Boot Application

Use **Spring Initializr** with these dependencies:

xml

CopyEdit

```xml
<dependencies>
   <!-- Spring Web for REST APIs -->
   <dependency>
      <groupId>org.springframework.boot</groupId>
      <artifactId>spring-boot-starter-web</artifactId>
   </dependency>

   <!-- Spring Data JPA for Database -->
   <dependency>
      <groupId>org.springframework.boot</groupId>
      <artifactId>spring-boot-starter-data-jpa</artifactId>
   </dependency>

   <!-- H2 Database for Development -->
   <dependency>
```

```xml
      <groupId>com.h2database</groupId>
      <artifactId>h2</artifactId>
      <scope>runtime</scope>
   </dependency>

   <!-- Spring Security for Authentication -->
   <dependency>
      <groupId>org.springframework.boot</groupId>
      <artifactId>spring-boot-starter-security</artifactId>
   </dependency>

   <!-- WebSockets -->
   <dependency>
      <groupId>org.springframework.boot</groupId>
      <artifactId>spring-boot-starter-websocket</artifactId>
   </dependency>

   <!-- Messaging with STOMP -->
   <dependency>
      <groupId>org.springframework.boot</groupId>
      <artifactId>spring-boot-starter-messaging</artifactId>
   </dependency>
</dependencies>
```

1.2 Configure Database in application.properties

properties

CopyEdit

```properties
spring.datasource.url=jdbc:h2:mem:social
spring.datasource.driverClassName=org.h2.Driver
spring.datasource.username=sa
spring.datasource.password=
spring.jpa.database-platform=org.hibernate.dialect.H2Dialect
```

274

spring.h2.console.enabled=true

Step 2: Implementing Real-Time Notifications

2.1 Define the Notification Entity

java

CopyEdit

```java
package com.social.model;

import jakarta.persistence.*;
import lombok.*;

import java.time.LocalDateTime;

@Entity
@Getter @Setter @NoArgsConstructor @AllArgsConstructor
public class Notification {

    @Id
    @GeneratedValue(strategy = GenerationType.IDENTITY)
    private Long id;

    private String message;
    private boolean seen = false;

    @ManyToOne
    private User recipient;

    private LocalDateTime timestamp = LocalDateTime.now();
}
```

2.2 Create the NotificationRepository

java

CopyEdit

```java
package com.social.repository;

import com.social.model.Notification;
import org.springframework.data.jpa.repository.JpaRepository;
import java.util.List;

public interface NotificationRepository extends JpaRepository<Notification, Long> {
    List<Notification> findByRecipientIdAndSeenFalse(Long recipientId);
}
```

2.3 Implement WebSocket Configuration

WebSocketConfig.java:

java

CopyEdit

```java
package com.social.config;

import org.springframework.context.annotation.Configuration;
import org.springframework.messaging.simp.config.MessageBrokerRegistry;
import org.springframework.web.socket.config.annotation.EnableWebSocketMessageBroker;
import org.springframework.web.socket.config.annotation.StompEndpointRegistry;
import org.springframework.web.socket.config.annotation.WebSocketMessageBrokerConfigurer;

@Configuration
@EnableWebSocketMessageBroker
public class WebSocketConfig implements WebSocketMessageBrokerConfigurer {

    @Override
```

```java
    public void registerStompEndpoints(StompEndpointRegistry registry) {
        registry.addEndpoint("/ws").setAllowedOrigins("*").withSockJS();
    }

    @Override
    public void configureMessageBroker(MessageBrokerRegistry registry) {
        registry.enableSimpleBroker("/topic");
        registry.setApplicationDestinationPrefixes("/app");
    }
}
```

2.4 Create the NotificationService

java

CopyEdit

```java
package com.social.service;

import com.social.model.Notification;
import com.social.repository.NotificationRepository;
import org.springframework.messaging.simp.SimpMessagingTemplate;
import org.springframework.stereotype.Service;

import java.util.List;

@Service
public class NotificationService {

    private final NotificationRepository notificationRepository;
    private final SimpMessagingTemplate messagingTemplate;

    public NotificationService(NotificationRepository notificationRepository,
SimpMessagingTemplate messagingTemplate) {
        this.notificationRepository = notificationRepository;
```

277

```java
        this.messagingTemplate = messagingTemplate;
    }

    public void sendNotification(Notification notification) {
        notificationRepository.save(notification);
        messagingTemplate.convertAndSend("/topic/notifications/" +
notification.getRecipient().getId(), notification);
    }

    public List<Notification> getUnreadNotifications(Long userId) {
        return notificationRepository.findByRecipientIdAndSeenFalse(userId);
    }
}
```

2.5 Create the NotificationController

java

CopyEdit

```java
package com.social.controller;

import com.social.model.Notification;
import com.social.service.NotificationService;
import org.springframework.web.bind.annotation.*;

import java.util.List;

@RestController
@RequestMapping("/api/notifications")
public class NotificationController {

    private final NotificationService notificationService;

    public NotificationController(NotificationService notificationService) {
```

```java
        this.notificationService = notificationService;
    }

    @GetMapping("/{userId}")
    public List<Notification> getUnreadNotifications(@PathVariable Long userId) {
        return notificationService.getUnreadNotifications(userId);
    }
}
```

Step 3: Implementing Real-Time Messaging

3.1 Define the Message Entity

java
CopyEdit

```java
package com.social.model;

import jakarta.persistence.*;
import lombok.*;

import java.time.LocalDateTime;

@Entity
@Getter @Setter @NoArgsConstructor @AllArgsConstructor
public class Message {

    @Id
    @GeneratedValue(strategy = GenerationType.IDENTITY)
    private Long id;

    private String content;

    @ManyToOne
```

```java
    private User sender;

    @ManyToOne
    private User receiver;

    private LocalDateTime timestamp = LocalDateTime.now();
}
```

3.2 Create the MessageService

java

CopyEdit

```java
package com.social.service;

import com.social.model.Message;
import com.social.repository.MessageRepository;
import org.springframework.messaging.simp.SimpMessagingTemplate;
import org.springframework.stereotype.Service;

@Service
public class MessageService {

    private final MessageRepository messageRepository;
    private final SimpMessagingTemplate messagingTemplate;

    public MessageService(MessageRepository messageRepository, SimpMessagingTemplate messagingTemplate) {
        this.messageRepository = messageRepository;
        this.messagingTemplate = messagingTemplate;
    }

    public void sendMessage(Message message) {
        messageRepository.save(message);
```

```java
        messagingTemplate.convertAndSend("/topic/messages/" +
message.getReceiver().getId(), message);
    }
}
```

3.3 Create the MessageController

java

CopyEdit

```java
package com.social.controller;

import com.social.model.Message;
import com.social.service.MessageService;
import org.springframework.web.bind.annotation.*;

@RestController
@RequestMapping("/api/messages")
public class MessageController {

    private final MessageService messageService;

    public MessageController(MessageService messageService) {
        this.messageService = messageService;
    }

    @PostMapping
    public void sendMessage(@RequestBody Message message) {
        messageService.sendMessage(message);
    }
}
```

Step 4: Setting Up the React Frontend

4.1 Install Dependencies

bash

CopyEdit

```
npm install @stomp/stompjs axios react-router-dom
```

4.2 Create WebSocket Connection in src/websocket.js

javascript

CopyEdit

```javascript
import { Client } from "@stomp/stompjs";

const client = new Client({
  brokerURL: "ws://localhost:8080/ws",
});

export const subscribeToNotifications = (userId, callback) => {
  client.onConnect = () => {
    client.subscribe(`/topic/notifications/${userId}`, (message) => {
      callback(JSON.parse(message.body));
    });
  };
  client.activate();
};
```

4.3 Create NotificationComponent.js

javascript

CopyEdit

```javascript
import React, { useEffect, useState } from "react";
import { subscribeToNotifications } from "../websocket";
```

```
const NotificationComponent = ({ userId }) => {
  const [notifications, setNotifications] = useState([]);

  useEffect(() => {
    subscribeToNotifications(userId, (notification) => {
      setNotifications((prev) => [...prev, notification]);
    });
  }, [userId]);

  return (
    <div>
      <h3>Notifications</h3>
      {notifications.map((notif, index) => (
        <p key={index}>{notif.message}</p>
      ))}
    </div>
  );
};

export default NotificationComponent;
```

■ **Real-Time Notifications** with WebSockets.

■ **Messaging System** for private chats.

■ **React Frontend for Live Updates.**

■ Next, we will add **authentication and deploy the full system to a cloud platform (AWS, GCP, or Firebase).**

Designing an Interactive User Interface & Using WebSockets for Live Updates

In this section, we will design an **interactive user interface** for our **real-time social media dashboard** using **React and Material-UI**. We will also integrate **WebSockets (STOMP over SockJS)** to enable **live updates** for notifications and messaging.

Step 1: Setting Up the React UI

1.1 Install UI Dependencies

bash

CopyEdit

```
npm install @mui/material @mui/icons-material @emotion/react @emotion/styled
react-router-dom axios @stomp/stompjs sockjs-client
```

- **Material-UI** for UI components.
- **React Router** for navigation.
- **Axios** for API calls.
- **STOMP + SockJS** for WebSocket communication.

1.2 Structuring the Frontend

Create the following **folder structure** inside src/:

css

CopyEdit

```
src/
|── components/
|    ├── Navbar.js
|    ├── Notifications.js
|    ├── Chat.js
```

```
| — pages/
|   ├── Home.js
|   ├── Messages.js
| — websocket/
|   ├── WebSocketClient.js
| — App.js
| — index.js
```

Step 2: Setting Up WebSockets in React

2.1 Create WebSocket Client

Create src/websocket/WebSocketClient.js:

javascript
CopyEdit
```javascript
import { Client } from "@stomp/stompjs";
import SockJS from "sockjs-client";

let stompClient = null;

export const connectWebSocket = (userId, onNotification, onMessage) => {
  const socket = new SockJS("http://localhost:8080/ws");
  stompClient = new Client({
    webSocketFactory: () => socket,
    onConnect: () => {
      console.log("Connected to WebSocket");

      // Subscribe to notifications
      stompClient.subscribe(`/topic/notifications/${userId}`, (message) => {
        onNotification(JSON.parse(message.body));
      });
```

```javascript
    // Subscribe to messages
    stompClient.subscribe(`/topic/messages/${userId}`, (message) => {
      onMessage(JSON.parse(message.body));
    });
  },
});

  stompClient.activate();
};

export const sendMessage = (message) => {
  if (stompClient && stompClient.connected) {
    stompClient.publish({ destination: "/app/chat", body: JSON.stringify(message) });
  }
};
```

Step 3: Building the Interactive UI

3.1 Create the Navbar Component

src/components/Navbar.js:

javascript
CopyEdit

```javascript
import React from "react";
import { AppBar, Toolbar, Typography, IconButton } from "@mui/material";
import NotificationsIcon from "@mui/icons-material/Notifications";
import ChatIcon from "@mui/icons-material/Chat";
import { useNavigate } from "react-router-dom";

const Navbar = () => {
  const navigate = useNavigate();
```

```jsx
  return (
    <AppBar position="static">
      <Toolbar>
        <Typography variant="h6" style={{ flexGrow: 1 }}>Social
Dashboard</Typography>
        <IconButton color="inherit" onClick={() => navigate("/messages")}>
          <ChatIcon />
        </IconButton>
        <IconButton color="inherit" onClick={() => navigate("/notifications")}>
          <NotificationsIcon />
        </IconButton>
      </Toolbar>
    </AppBar>
  );
};

export default Navbar;
```

3.2 Create the Notifications Component

src/components/Notifications.js:

javascript
CopyEdit
```javascript
import React, { useEffect, useState } from "react";
import { connectWebSocket } from "../websocket/WebSocketClient";
import { List, ListItem, ListItemText, Typography, Container } from "@mui/material";

const Notifications = ({ userId }) => {
  const [notifications, setNotifications] = useState([]);

  useEffect(() => {
    connectWebSocket(userId, (notification) => {
```

```
      setNotifications((prev) => [notification, ...prev]);
    }, () => {});

  }, [userId]);

  return (
    <Container>
      <Typography variant="h5">Notifications</Typography>
      <List>
        {notifications.map((notif, index) => (
          <ListItem key={index}>
            <ListItemText primary={notif.message} secondary={notif.timestamp} />
          </ListItem>
        ))}
      </List>
    </Container>
  );
};

export default Notifications;
```

3.3 Create the Chat Component

src/components/Chat.js:

javascript

CopyEdit

```
import React, { useState, useEffect } from "react";
import { connectWebSocket, sendMessage } from "../websocket/WebSocketClient";
import { Container, TextField, Button, List, ListItem, ListItemText } from "@mui/material";

const Chat = ({ userId }) => {
  const [messages, setMessages] = useState([]);
```

```
const [message, setMessage] = useState("");

useEffect(() => {
  connectWebSocket(userId, () => {}, (msg) => {
    setMessages((prev) => [...prev, msg]);
  });
}, [userId]);

const handleSend = () => {
  if (message.trim()) {
    sendMessage({ senderId: userId, content: message });
    setMessage("");
  }
};

return (
  <Container>
    <h3>Chat</h3>
    <List>
      {messages.map((msg, index) => (
        <ListItem key={index}>
          <ListItemText primary={msg.content} />
        </ListItem>
      ))}
    </List>
    <TextField
      fullWidth
      value={message}
      onChange={(e) => setMessage(e.target.value)}
      placeholder="Type a message..."
    />
    <Button onClick={handleSend}>Send</Button>
  </Container>
);
```

```
};

export default Chat;
```

3.4 Set Up Routing

Modify src/App.js:

javascript
CopyEdit
```javascript
import React from "react";
import { BrowserRouter as Router, Routes, Route } from "react-router-dom";
import Navbar from "./components/Navbar";
import Notifications from "./components/Notifications";
import Chat from "./components/Chat";

const App = () => {
  const userId = 1; // Simulating a logged-in user

  return (
    <Router>
      <Navbar />
      <Routes>
        <Route path="/notifications" element={<Notifications userId={userId} />} />
        <Route path="/messages" element={<Chat userId={userId} />} />
      </Routes>
    </Router>
  );
};

export default App;
```

Step 4: Testing WebSockets

4.1 Start the Spring Boot Server

bash

CopyEdit

```
mvn spring-boot:run
```

4.2 Start the React Frontend

bash

CopyEdit

```
npm start
```

4.3 Test WebSocket Functionality

1. Open two browser tabs.
2. Navigate to /messages and send a message.
3. The second tab should receive the message **in real-time**.
4. Similarly, notifications should appear in **real-time** when triggered.

Step 5: Enhancing the UI

5.1 Improve Chat with User Avatars

Modify Chat.js:

javascript

CopyEdit

```
import { Avatar } from "@mui/material";

<ListItem key={index}>
  <Avatar>{msg.senderId}</Avatar>
  <ListItemText primary={msg.content} />
</ListItem>
```

5.2 Add Notification Count in Navbar

Modify Navbar.js:

javascript

CopyEdit

```
import Badge from "@mui/material/Badge";

<Badge badgeContent={notifications.length} color="secondary">
    <NotificationsIcon />
</Badge>
```

5.3 Show Online Users

1. Store **online users in a state** using WebSocket.
2. Display **online status in chat**.

javascript

CopyEdit

```
<ListItem key={index}>
    <Avatar style={{ backgroundColor: onlineUsers.includes(msg.senderId) ? "green" : "gray"
}}>{msg.senderId}</Avatar>
    <ListItemText primary={msg.content} />
</ListItem>
```

■ **Designed a real-time social media UI** with Material-UI.

■ **Integrated WebSockets** for instant notifications and messaging.

■ **Built a responsive and interactive dashboard.**

■ **Next Steps:**

292

- Implement user authentication (JWT).
- Deploy the full-stack app on AWS/GCP.

Chapter 17: Appendices

This chapter provides **quick reference guides** for Spring Boot, React, and HTTP status codes. It also includes **additional learning resources**, GitHub links, and answers to frequently asked questions.

Cheat Sheets

1. Spring Boot Annotations Cheat Sheet

Annotation	Description
@SpringBootApplication	Entry point for a Spring Boot application. Combines @Configuration , @EnableAutoConfiguration , and @ComponentScan .
@RestController	Marks a class as a RESTful controller, returning JSON responses.
@GetMapping , @PostMapping , @PutMapping , @DeleteMapping	Maps HTTP methods (GET , POST , PUT , DELETE) to specific controller methods.
@RequestParam	Extracts query parameters from a URL.
@PathVariable	Extracts path variables from a URL.
@RequestBody	Converts JSON request body to a Java object.
@Autowired	Injects dependencies automatically.
@Service	Marks a class as a service layer component.
@Repository	Marks a class as a database repository.
@Entity	Defines a JPA entity mapped to a database table.
@Transactional	Wraps a method in a database transaction.
@ExceptionHandler	Handles specific exceptions at the controller level.
@EnableWebSocketMessageBroker	Enables WebSocket support in Spring Boot.
@Cacheable	Caches method results to improve performance.

2. React Hooks Cheat Sheet

Hook	Description
useState	Manages state in functional components.
useEffect	Handles side effects (e.g., API calls, event listeners).
useContext	Accesses global state without passing props manually.
useReducer	Alternative to useState for complex state management.
useRef	Maintains a reference to a DOM element or mutable value.
useMemo	Optimizes expensive calculations by memoizing values.
useCallback	Memoizes callback functions to prevent unnecessary re-renders.
useNavigate	Redirects users to different routes in react-router-dom.
useParams	Accesses URL parameters in React Router.

Example: Using useState and useEffect

javascript

CopyEdit

```javascript
import React, { useState, useEffect } from "react";

const Counter = () => {
  const [count, setCount] = useState(0);

  useEffect(() => {
    console.log("Component mounted or updated");
  }, [count]);

  return (
    <div>
      <h1>Count: {count}</h1>
      <button onClick={() => setCount(count + 1)}>Increment</button>
    </div>
  );
};

export default Counter;
```

3. HTTP Status Codes Cheat Sheet

Status Code	Meaning
200 OK	Successful request.
201 Created	Resource created successfully.
204 No Content	Request successful, but no response body.
400 Bad Request	Invalid request from the client.
401 Unauthorized	Authentication required.
403 Forbidden	Client does not have permission.
404 Not Found	Resource not found.
409 Conflict	Request conflicts with existing resource.
500 Internal Server Error	Unexpected error on the server.
502 Bad Gateway	Server received an invalid response from an upstream server.
503 Service Unavailable	Server is temporarily down or overloaded.

Additional Learning Resources and GitHub Links

1. Spring Boot Documentation & Tutorials

- Spring Boot Official Docs
- Spring Security Guide
- REST API Best Practices

2. React Documentation & Learning Resources

- React Official Docs
- React Router Guide
- Material-UI Docs

3. WebSockets & Real-Time Communication

- STOMP Protocol Guide
- Using WebSockets in Spring Boot

4. Deployment & Cloud

- <u>AWS EC2 Setup for Spring Boot</u>
- Deploying React Apps to Vercel

Frequently Asked Questions (FAQs)

1. Why use Spring Boot for backend development?

Spring Boot simplifies backend development by providing built-in features for database access, security, caching, and real-time communication. It minimizes configuration overhead and supports REST APIs, WebSockets, and microservices.

2. What is the best way to structure a full-stack project?

A recommended structure:

scss

CopyEdit

```
full-stack-app/
|— backend/ (Spring Boot)
|   ├— src/main/java/com/app/
|   |   ├— controller/
|   |   ├— service/
|   |   ├— repository/
|   |   ├— model/
|— frontend/ (React)
|   ├— src/
|   |   ├— components/
|   |   ├— pages/
|   |   ├— redux/
```

3. How do I handle authentication between React and Spring Boot?

1. Use **JWT authentication** in Spring Boot.
2. Store the JWT token in **localStorage** or **httpOnly cookies** in React.
3. Send the token in Authorization headers for protected API requests.

Example API Request with Token:

javascript

CopyEdit

```
axios.get("/api/protected-route", {
  headers: { Authorization: `Bearer ${localStorage.getItem("token")}` }
});
```

4. How do I deploy a Spring Boot backend and React frontend together?

- **Option 1:** Deploy separately
    1. Host **React** on **Vercel/Netlify**
    2. Host **Spring Boot** on **AWS/GCP/DigitalOcean**
    3. Configure CORS to allow frontend requests.
- **Option 2:** Serve React from Spring Boot

Build React frontend:

bash

CopyEdit

```
npm run build
```

1.
2. Move the build/ folder to src/main/resources/static/ in Spring Boot.
3. Spring Boot will now serve React on /.

5. How can I improve the performance of my full-stack app?

- **Backend Optimization**
    - Use **Spring Cache (Redis)** for frequently accessed data.
    - Optimize SQL queries with **indexes** and **pagination**.
    - Enable **Gzip compression** in Spring Boot.
- **Frontend Optimization**

- Use **lazy loading** and **code splitting** in React.
- Optimize images with **WebP format**.
- Use **Redux Toolkit** for efficient state management.

6. How do I monitor errors in production?

- **Backend:** Use **Spring Boot Actuator** for health monitoring.
- **Frontend:** Use **Sentry or LogRocket** to track client-side errors.
- **Logs:** Store application logs in **Elasticsearch + Kibana** for better analysis.

Conclusion

This **Appendices chapter** serves as a **quick reference guide** for **Spring Boot, React, WebSockets, and HTTP status codes**. It also provides **learning resources, best practices, and troubleshooting tips** to help developers enhance their **full-stack development workflow**.

■ If you're looking to expand your skills further, consider learning **GraphQL, Kubernetes, Serverless Architecture, and CI/CD automation with GitHub Actions.** 🚀

www.ingramcontent.com/pod-product-compliance
Lightning Source LLC
La Vergne TN
LVHW051433050326
832903LV00030BD/3058